Why Marriages Do Not Last

Why Marriages Do Not Last

(Based on True Stories)

Sandra Goodlight

AuthorHouse™
1663 Liberty Drive
Bloomington, IN 47403
www.authorhouse.com
Phone: 1-800-839-8640

First Edition 2012
Cover design by AuthorHouse

ISBN: 978-1-4678-7943-9 (sc)
ISBN: 978-1-4678-7944-6 (ebk)

Printed in the United States of America

Any people depicted in stock imagery provided by Thinkstock are models, and such images are being used for illustrative purposes only.
Certain stock imagery © Thinkstock.

This book is printed on acid-free paper.

This book is based on true stories, and the people mentioned in the book are named by only the first letter of their name, first name or full name.

The Bible chapters and verses are taken from the New King James Version.

The author believes that this book will not only help you find the right spouse or solve your marriage problems, but also will help you to have a genuine relationship with God.

This book is dedicated to all married and single men and women wishing for healthy and winning marriages.

Contents

INTRODUCTION xv

A. The Order of the Book: Why Marriages Do Not Last xv

B. Divorce Rates for Ten Countries xvi
   1. Australia xvi
   2. Brazil xvii
   3. Canada xviii
   4. China xviii
   5. Germany xix
   6. India xx
   7. Japan xx
   8. Korea xx
   9. United States of America xxi
   10. United Kingdom xxii

C. Men Prefer to Cohabit xxiii

D. Choosing a Spouse xxiv

E. The Causes of Marriage Breakdown xxiv
   Story 1 xxviii
   Story 2 xxviii
   Story 3 xxix
   Story 4 xxxi
   Story 5 xxxi
   Story 6 xxxiii
   Story 7 xxxvi
   Story 8 xxxvi
   Story 9 xxxviii
   Story 10 xxxviii

F. The Two Important Questions xxxix

I. Does He Love You? 1

    A. This Is True Love 2

    B. The Man Who Loves You Treats You Well.............................3

    Story 1 3

    C. The Man Who Loves You Communicates
       and Listens to You 3

    D. The Man Who Loves You Fellowships with You 4

    E. The Man Who Loves You Does Not Make
       You Feel Unhappy 5

    Story 2 5

    F. The Man Who Loves You Does Not Leave You
       for Someone Else...6

    Story 3 6

    Story 4 6

    Story 5 7

II. Is He the Right One? 11

    A. The Right One Is Chosen by God 11

    B. The Right One Is the Bone of Your Bones and
       the Flesh of Your Flesh 12

    C. The Right One Is Not Afraid of Commitment 12

    D. The Right One Knows Your Dos and Don'ts......................13

    E. The Right One Knows His Image 13

    F. The Right One Is Very Supportive 14

    G. The Right One Is Cultivated 14

    H. The Right One Does Not Reject You 15

    I. The Right One Does Not Judge You 15

    J. The Right One Is Always There When You Need Him 16

K. The Right One Sticks Closer 17

L. The Right One Sees Marriage as an Honour 17

III. Love at First Sight 21

Story 1 21

Story 2 23

IV. Lack of Communication 29

Story 1 30

Story 2 33

V. Alcohol 39

Story 1 41

Story 2 41

Story 3 44

Story 4 45

Story 5 45

Story 6 46

Story 7 47

VI. Love of Money 53

Story 1 55

Story 2 56

Story 3 59

VII. Lack of Love and Care 67

Story 1 71

Story 2 73

Story 3 77

Story 4 80

Story 5 81

VIII. Religions 85

    Story 1 92

    Story 2 93

    Story 3 99

    Story 4 101

    Story 5 105

    Story 6 107

    Story 7 108

IX. Domestic Violence 113

    Story 1 115

    Story 2 117

    Story 3 118

    Story 4 119

    Story 5 120

X. In-Laws 127

    Story 1 128

    Story 2 129

    Story 3 130

    Story 4 132

    Story 5 133

    Story 6 133

    Story 7 134

    Story 8 137

    Story 9 138

CONCLUSION 141

Acknowledgements

To God Almighty: thank you for the extraordinary gift and wisdom that you have bestowed upon me through your Son, Jesus Christ. Your love and grace through the Holy Spirit have facilitated me from the beginning to complete this book.

INTRODUCTION

A. The Order of the Book: Why Marriages Do Not Last

Five years ago, God ordered me to write this book. I ignored the Word of God because I was more focused on pursuing a career in law. Ever since I refused to do what God commanded me to do, I faced challenges and difficulties. One day, I asked God, 'Why do I struggle in everything I do?' The Almighty God reminded me of the disobedience of Jonah. I took my Bible immediately and began to read the book of Jonah. Whilst reading it, God said to me, 'If Jonah had not gone to Nineveh to preach to the people of that city, the people would not have turned away from their evil but would have perished because of Jonah's disobedience.' Since that day, I have collaborated with God to ensure that this book is written and published according to His will.

Marriage is a gift from God that should not be taken for granted. Marriage is the right atmosphere to engage in sexual relations and to build a family life. Marriage is a public declaration of love and commitment. When God created Adam, He knew that it was not good for him to be alone; He formed Eve and gave her to Adam as a wife. God could have chosen not to create Eve, but His desire was for a man and woman to be joined in holy matrimony and live happily ever.

The first marriage problem God commanded me to write about was alcohol. There are other marriage issues that He commanded me to write about, but not all of them made it in this book and will appear in future volumes.

xvi • Sandra Goodlight

B. Divorce Rates for Ten Countries

The divorce rate has been staying high in lots of European countries and in America, and many Asian countries are catching up. For example, the divorce rate of Korea has ranked third in the world, and the United States of America has the highest rate of divorce in the world.

1. Australia

The numbers of divorces granted in Australia have been decreasing each year since reaching a peak in 2001, according to the Australia Bureau of Statistics. This trend continued in 2007 with 47,963 divorces granted in comparison to 51,375 in 2006, showing a decrease of 3,412 or 6.6% over this period. The number of divorces granted in 2007 was 9.8% lower than five years ago, but only 6.6% lower than 10 years ago due to a peak in the number of divorces granted in 2001.

In 2007, the crude divorce rate was 2.3 people granted divorce per 1,000 estimated residents, declining from 2.5 in 2006. Of all females who were granted a divorce in 2007, 62.3 per cent were aged less than forty-five years. In comparison, only 52.5 per cent of males granted a divorce were in this age group. The median age for males granted divorce in 2007 was 44.2 years, compared with 41.3 years for females.

The proportion of divorces involving children under the age of 18 years has been decreasing, although this decline has slowed in recent years. The proportion of divorces involving children was 49.3% in 2007. The number of children affected by divorce has also decreased from 48,396 in 2006 to 44,371 in 2007, and is similar to the number of children recorded over twenty years ago.

The median age at divorce has been increasing steadily for both males and females over the past twenty years. This trend continued in 2007, with the median age increasing by 0.3 years for males and 0.2 years for females. The rise in the median age may be attributed to the increasing age at marriage, may be the increase in the interval between marriage and divorce, and could be reflective of the overall ageing of the Australian population.

As for females, age-specific divorce rates in 2007 were highest for the thirty-five to thirty-nine years old, while among males it was highest for the forty to forty-four years old. This difference may reflect the tendency for females to marry at a younger age than males.

In 2007, the median length of marriage to separation was 8.9 years; in comparison, the median length of marriage to separation in 2003 was 8.7 years, and in 1998 it was 7.8 years. The median length of marriage to divorce was 12.5 years for divorces granted in 2007. In 2003, it was 12.2 years, and in 1998 it was 11.2 years. Median length of marriage to both separation and divorce has been steadily increasing over the last twenty years, although the length of marriage to divorce has been increasing at a slightly faster rate than length of marriage to separation.

The difference between median length of marriage to separation and divorce was 3.6 years in 2007, compared with 3.5 years in 2003 and 3.4 years in 1998.

Over the last twenty years, the proportion of joint applications for divorce has been increasing, while the proportion of applications by only the male or female has decreased. This trend has continued in 2007, with decreases of 2.0 and 1.3 percentage points, respectively, on the proportion of applications lodged by the male or female only. Conversely, the proportion of joint applications has increased by 3.4 percentage points in 2007.

2. Brazil

The divorce rate in Brazil has increased to twice as much as 1985, which may be due to the removal of the law that a man can only divorce twice in his life. Women are more open about divorce in Brazil now. The statistics show that 73 per cent of the divorce or separation cases are raised by women at first. Besides, the loyalty of men is a direct reason for the breakup of the marriage. There is a strange phenomenon in Brazil that more and more single girls like to seek married men.

In order to keep the stability of society, the Brazilian law states that the couples can get divorced only after two years of marriage, and two years of separation is required. It also regulates that people can't get remarried until two years after the divorce. Despite the fact that the process of divorce takes a long time, people are still committed to getting divorces, given the doubling of the number since 1985.

3. Canada

The divorce rate in Canada is about 48 per cent. Almost 75 per cent of Canadian divorces are being initiated by women. One year after separation or divorce, 50 per cent of children of divorced or separated families never see their fathers again. First marriages have about a 50 per cent chance of ending in divorce, and that risk becomes greater with each successive marriage (about 72 per cent for second marriages, and about 85 per cent for third marriages).

The percentage of divorced men and women who remarry is about 75 per cent and 65 per cent, respectively. The probability of remarriage between the years of thirty-five to fifty for women is 48 per cent, compared to 61 per cent for men. As for people between the age of twenty-five and thirty-five, the probability is 66 per cent for women and close to 80 per cent among men.

4. China

According to the statistics of China Civil Administration Department, there were 341,000 divorces in 1980, 800,000 in 1990, 1,210,000 in 2000, and 1,331,000 in 2005; clearly the rate of divorce has rapidly increased.

Xu Anqi, analyst of Shanghai Social Science Academy and standing director of China Research Association for Women and Family, says the reasons for the rise of divorces in China vary. First, the transferring period of society has a great impact on the stability of marriage. Second, along with the improvement of life conditions, people have higher expectation about marriage quality and about love. Third, the simplification of marriage and the divorce procedure also makes divorce easier. Xu Anqi believes that the high divorce rate of a certain area doesn't mean there is a low quality of marriage or an unstable society. A marriage survey reveals that people feel happier in a more open country with loose divorce laws because the couples with problem could break up easily, and along ones with stable relationships, that leads to high quality of life and a more harmonious social status.

Chen Xinxin, from Women Studies Institute of ACWF (All-China Women's Federation), also thinks that the improvement of women's social status is one of the reasons for a growing divorce rate. Women are becoming more and more independent economically and spiritually, and this is reflected by the liberation of women and social progress.

5. Germany

The divorce rate stays high in Germany in recent years. The statistics show that over two hundred thousand couples divorced last year. The German media charge this to the rising of unemployment. The popular 'divorce economy', including divorce-related magazines, companies, bars, and TV shows, also adds fuel to the fire. All kinds of social institutions in Germany have to take over the responsibility for broken families, which costs a lot to the country. A German marriage law expert says, 'The divorced couples should consider the duty and responsibility for their elders, children, family, and society at any time.'

In actuality, the problem of single-parent families, the elders, and the children's education caused by hasty divorce has become a crucial social problem. Therefore, German legislative organizations are trying to make it more difficult to divorce. Divorce is not encouraged by the German government; once the husband wants to get divorced, he has to give half of the income to his wife for the rest of his life.

6. India

In India, the divorce rate is similar to what it was ten years ago. There has been no formal statistics about divorce rate due to the large number of rural residents and an incomplete divorce system, but it is widely acknowledged that the country has a great increase of divorce rate. The divorce of young people is a basic cause of the rising of the divorce rate. The phenomenon of 'family group marriage' is also worthy to note. In the rural area of India, family marriage is quite common. For instance, the brothers of one family may marry the sisters of another family at the same time. In this case, the problem and divorce of one marriage would always end with group divorce.

According to the National Statistics data, the higher educational level that women have, the less likely they are to divorce their spouses.

7. Japan

In Japan, divorces were on a generally upward trend from the 1960s until 2002, when they hit a peak of 290,000. Since then, both the number of divorces and the divorce rate have declined for six years straight. In 2008, the number of divorces totaled 251,000, and the divorce rate was 1.99 per 1,000 people.

8. Korea

Korea's divorce rate ranks third in the world after American and the United Kingdom, and according to the statistics of Korean government, the divorce rate in Korea raises at an average speed of 0.5 per cent every year. In the past ten years, the total amount has increased three times. That is to say, there are 2.8 marriages breaking up in every thousand people.

The relationship between mother-in-law and daughter-in-law is the vital reason in divorce cases in Korea. Divorce cases always increase after mid-autumn day, New Year's, or summer holiday; this may be because couples quarrel after the family gets together, and then the problem gets worse. One more reason is the change of value. In addition, more women raise the proposal of divorce or separation (66.7 per cent), and about 46.4 per cent of the divorce cases are because one spouse is having an affair. In order to stop the growing number of divorces, the Korean government has taken measures such as the adoption of a 'thinking period' and a voluntary intercession system. These measures have proved to be effective according to some relevant statistics.

9. United States of America

In 2008, 46 per cent of all marriages involve a remarriage for one or both spouses. It is estimated that 40 per cent of all marriages ended in divorce as of 2008. On average, first marriages that end in divorce last about eight years. Of the first marriages for women from 1955 to 1959, about 79 per cent reached their fifteenth anniversary, compared with only 57 per cent for women who married for the first time from 1985 to 1989.

Statistics show that 50 per cent of all US marriages end in divorce. This is comprised of various age groups, and it seems the younger the brides and grooms, the more likely it is to end. Couples twenty-nine years of age and under had a much higher failure rate than those thirty years of age and older. Could this be because the older couples are more matured and experienced? Or is it due to the fact that older couples wait a bit longer before they get married? Statistics show that it is good to wait until one is a little older and know what one wants in life before taking the big leap.

Statistics show that 27.6 per cent of marriages for women under the age of twenty end in divorce, and for men it is 11.7 per cent. Statistics also show that women and men between the ages of twenty and thirty-nine end their marriages in divorce. Women between the ages of twenty and twenty-four are at 36.6 per cent, and the men are 38.8 per cent. Women between the ages of twenty-five to twenty-nine are 16.4 per cent; and the men are 22.3 per cent. The divorce rate for women between the ages of thirty to thirty-four is 8.5 per cent, and the men are at 11.6 per cent. Women between the ages of thirty-five to thirty-nine get divorced 5.15 per cent of the time, while the men are at 6.5 per cent.

According to Jennifer Baker of the Forest Institute of Professional Psychology in Springfield, Missouri, 50 per cent percent of first marriages, 67 per cent of second and 74 per cent of third marriages end in divorce. The *Enrichment Journal* stated that the divorce rate in America for first marriage is 41 per cent, for second marriage is 60 per cent and for third marriage is 73 per cent.

10. United Kingdom

Britain has 2.7 divorces per 1,000 citizens, compared with a European average of 1.8, according to government figures in the study. Italy had the lowest rate at 0.6 divorces, while Spain registered 0.9, France 2.0, Austria 2.2, Germany 2.3, and Finland 2.7.

The provisional number of divorces in the United Kingdom fell by 2.6 per cent last year to 144,220 (from 148,141 in 2006). The provisional number fell by 1.9 per cent in Scotland, from 13,014 in 2006 to 12,773 last year, but it rose by 14 per cent in Northern Ireland to 2,913, from 2,565 in 2006.

The rate fell to 11.9 divorces per thousand married people in 2007—the lowest since 1981—compared to 12.2 per thousand in 2006, according to the Office for National Statistics. The number of divorces also fell for the fourth year in a row to 128,534—the lowest number since 1976 when there were 126,694. The rate of divorce was more than twice as high for men and women aged twenty-five to twenty-nine, the group with the highest divorce rate overall. Divorce rates also rose for men and women aged sixty and over, and for women aged forty-five to forty-nine. Last year there were 26.6 divorces per thousand for both women and men aged twenty-five to twenty-nine. A fifth of men and women divorcing last year also had a previous marriage that ended in divorce—a proportion that has doubled since 1980. More than half (51 per cent) of couples who divorced last year had at least one child under sixteen.

It is probably well-known that divorce rates have increased in the UK over many years. The National Statistics website shows us that over the period of 1971 to about 2003, divorce rates went up from six per one thousand married couples to about thirteen per one thousand, more than doubling. Over the last four years or so, the rate has consistently fallen to the 1981 level of about twelve per thousand—still double the old rates. However, the actual levels of divorce are relatively low. People in their late twenties have the highest divorce rates; this may be due to an increasingly casual approach to marriage from 'modern people.'

The report published by the Office for National Statistics show the number of divorce in England and Wales in 2009 was 113,949, a 6.4 per cent decrease since 2008 when there were 121,708, and the lowest since 1974. It is the sixth consecutive year that the number of divorces has fallen from a peak of 153,065 in 2003. However, the average age at divorce increased slightly for men and women in 2009, 44.0 for men in 2009 compared with 43.9 in 2008, and 41.5 for women compared with 41.4 in 2008.

What this tends to hide is the fact that in 2009, for the first time there were more single or cohabiting people in the UK than married people. This was an historic moment. There is no doubt that there has been a slow decline in the idea of marriage as a meaningful institution. The numbers of cohabiting people grew to such significant numbers that the laws in relation to 'divorcing' cohabiting couples was tightened up, as until recently these couples had to rely on a mish-mash of various laws such as contract and equitable principles to divide possessions, often including the home. Under these circumstances the women usually lost out.

C. Men Prefer to Cohabit

There is no doubt that the problems surrounding marriages have changed the way men embrace marriage. Men would rather cohabit than to marry, and women would prefer to marry because this would favour them and their children. The dream of every woman is to marry someday and live happily ever after, but due to the deceitful heart of the wicked, things do not normally turn out in the manner they should. Men should do the right thing, and should not allow the issues affecting marriages to put them off. Moreover, the will of God is for every man and woman to have a soul mate.

> *Search from the book of the Lord, and read: Not one of these shall fail; not one shall lack her mate. For My mouth has commanded it, and His Spirit has gathered them.*
> *—Isaiah 34:16*

D. Choosing a Spouse

Nowadays, choosing a spouse is like electing a president. The nation looks at the candidates' speech before deciding whom they want to be their president. When the president is selected and he fails to deliver as expected by the people, those who elected him will be dejected and disappointed. At this time, one thing they won't remember is that they elected him as their president because of his fine speech and not because he was the right person for the job. The same election mentality is also seen in individuals when they are selecting a spouse. The majority of men choose a spouse for the wrong reasons; they select a woman because of her outward looks and not because she is the right one for them.

> *Do not lust after her beauty in your heart, nor let her allure you with her eyelids.*
>
> *—Proverbs 6:25*

E. The Causes of Marriage Breakdown

Love at First Sight

Desiring to have a relationship with someone because of the person's personal appearance is caused by the lust of the eyes and the lust of the flesh. The lust of the eyes obviously refers to what is seen or what we want to see. The lust of the flesh often refers to unlawful desire which would lead to fornication or adultery. Men who are lured into marriage because of a woman's outward appearance do not always have successful relationships. This is because the relationship starts with an emotional condition that makes them feel romantic or sexual attraction for that stranger on the first encounter. Such a feeling is non-moral and, it constitutes a sinful act.

> *But I say to you that whoever looks at a woman to lust for her has already committed adultery with her in his heart.*
> —*Matthew 5:28*

> *I say then: Walk in the Spirit, and you shall not fulfil the lust of the flesh.*
> —*Galatians 5:16*

Lack of Communication

Communication is one of the keys to a successful and long-lasting relationship. Lack of communication between spouses makes a relationship unhealthy and unsuccessful. If your spouse does not communicate with you, you will feel lonely and isolated. When you are married, loneliness can seriously damage your marriage. The reason for this is because most people do not expect to feel lonely when they get married. Why should married couples feel lonely in their matrimonial home? They got married to be together with their spouse, and at the same time to beat the spirit of loneliness.

> *Again, if two lie down together, they will keep warm; but how can one be warm alone?*
> —*Ecclesiastes 4:11.*

The notion that an individual can become lonely in a committed relationship is often too painful to deal with. Once the realization is made, loneliness can cause all sorts of havoc, leading up to a partner's unfaithfulness, depression in one or both spouses, and bitterness and anger that eventually lead to divorce. To avoid this havoc, good spouses communicate healthily with their spouse. Good communication is important because it makes relationships work and helps put off loneliness.

Marriage is believed to be the most intimate of relationships. If married couples cannot communicate due to aloofness between them, their relationships will start to go wrong. Couples should not stand and watch their marriages destroyed because of the remoteness between them. Once they start to notice the coldness in their marriage, they should speak to their spouse and find out what is wrong. If their spouse is the kind that argues each time they want to speak to them, they ought to find another way to communicate to them.

Alcohol

There are some things that will not only harm you but will also prevent you from receiving from God. Alcohol is one of those things; it is a silent destroyer that ruins marriages and destroys lives. It takes over the good things that are part of a person's life. God did not create us to dwell on the earth without a purpose; He created each and every one of us with unique gifts, and for those gifts to manifest, we must be obedient to the Word of God. In the Scripture, God sometimes warned some parents before the birth of their child concerning things that could be a hindrance to the child's gift. Before John the Baptist's birth, for example, God warned his parents not to give him wine or strong (alcoholic) drink, 'For he will be great in the sight of the Lord, and shall drink neither wine nor strong drink. He will also be filled with the Holy Spirit, even from his mother's womb' (Luke 1:15). In the book of Judges, the angel of God warned Manoah, the mother of Samson, not to drink alcohol or eat anything unclean. Why? Because God knew she was about to carry a child with an extraordinary gift, and for the gift to manifest, Samson's mother must eschew from unclean food and drink.

Now therefore beware, I pray thee, and drink neither wine nor strong drink, and eat not any unclean thing.

—*Judges 13:4*

Many Christians cannot receive or hear from God because they are filled with alcohol. People who drink alcohol are unclean and are controlled by unclean spirits. According to the Scripture, those who are unclean will not enter the Kingdom of God (*'For this you know, that no whoremonger, nor unclean person, nor covetous man, who is an idolater, has any inheritance in the kingdom of Christ and of God'—Ephesians 5:5*). When a person is filled with alcohol, the unclean spirits make it difficult for the Holy Ghost to operate fully in that person, because the Light (Holy Spirit) and darkness (the devil) cannot perform together, and neither can they live in the same body. The Scripture says that our body is the temple of the Holy Ghost. In other words, the Spirit of God dwells in our body and controls it. But what happens when the Holy Spirit no longer lives in a person's body or controls it? The devil takes over, and when the devil controls a person's body and life, it will prevent the spiritual gift in that person from manifesting. Christians should not be filled with alcohol (the destroyer) but must be filled with the Holy Ghost (the redeemer).

> *Therefore do not be unwise, but understand what the will of the Lord is.*
>
> *—Ephesians 5:17*

> *And do not be drunk with wine, in which is dissipation [sin]; but be filled with the Spirit.*
>
> *—Ephesians 5:18*

Not only does alcohol prevent the manifestation of the gift of the Spirit, but it also causes more problems in the lives of those who drink it, especially in relationships and marriages. Many people complain about the abuse they received from an alcoholic spouse, and the stories they told about their abusive spouses were not surprising because a lot of people who drink abuse their spouse. Sometimes it is unwittingly because of the malfunction of their brain after consuming alcohol. Some people even end up killing their loved ones. In a marriage where alcohol is an issue, the marriage is unhealthy and the couple will not have a peaceful marital life.

Story 1

Ms S and Mr H were husband and wife. Before they got married, Mr H was not an alcoholic; he was just a very rude man with a nasty behaviour, and he never listened to anyone. His attitude became unbearable when he started to drink in large amounts, and his wife became so miserable and unhappy that she left him.

Story 2

Mr H and Ms W were married with four children. Mr H enjoyed alcohol and nearly killed himself when he had an accident due to his drinking. He did not learn from his mistakes and continued drinking as usual. When his wife couldn't handle his addiction, she walked out of their marriage and later filed for divorce.

These are real stories, and alcohol is the reason for the breakdown of these marriages. Alcohol is a marriage breaker and a silent killer. It can affect individuals in many ways: ranging from relatively minor consequences to incapacitation and even death. The disease potentially affects everything in a person's life, as the consequences of drinking snowball into bigger and bigger problems. Over the long run, things always get worse and never get better, unless the person decides to stop and turn around his or her life, like George W Bush did. The former president of the United State of America had to give up alcohol to stay in power. He spoke out about his agony concerning alcohol addiction, saying, 'I owe my presidency to giving up drinking.' (See the full story in chapter 5.)

Love of Money

It is not fictitious that many people, both male and female, get married for the love of money. They marry a rich person so that the spouse can provide them with tangible things that they want. For some people, money can buy anything—but money cannot buy love! You do not want to marry someone you do not love, especially when you have to spend the rest of your life with that person. It might seem like a nice life, being pampered and having money to buy everything that you want, but before money lures you to marriage, you should think carefully. Before you rush into marriage with that so-called millionaire, ask yourself these questions: How long will I pretend that I am in love? Can that person make me happy? When you are asking yourself these questions, I would like you to imagine that man or woman to be a person of deprived, unfortunate circumstances, and then ask yourself, 'Would I like to spend the rest of my life with such a person?' If your answer is no, then it is wrong if you marry because of the person's money, when you know he/she won't make you happy.

It is easy to pretend you love someone or that you are happy being in a relationship. But when you are married to someone, it is a different feeling, and one day your misery will come to light. Money can buy you a lot of things, but you would not want to spend the rest of your life with someone you do not love, just so you can buy things.

Money has become so important that men and women lie, cheat, bribe, defame, and kill to get it. The love of money becomes the ultimate idolatry. This is why Apostle Paul said, 'For the love of money is a root of all kinds of evil, for which some have strayed from the faith in their greediness, and pierced themselves through with many sorrows' (1 Tim. 6:10).

Story 3

When Ms D met Mr T, she told him that she had won a lottery but this was untrue. Ms D later lied to Mr T that she had cancer, this time seeking sympathy. She also tried to convince Mr T to move abroad with her. When she couldn't persuade him, she attacked him and tied his hands. When she went out to get a rod, Mr T managed to untie his hands. Ms D approached Mr T with a rod and tried to stab him, but Mr T got up immediately, and stopped her. Mr T thought this was one of Ms D's jokes and did not do anything about it.

The next day, a man came to possess Mr T's house. Mr T was shocked to hear that Ms D had gone behind his back and sold his property. This was when Mr T realised that Ms D meant to kill him, that this was not one of her jokes. He called the police and reported the incident, but the police did not believe him. Mr T did not give up; he continued to ask the police to do something about Ms D. Later, the police decided to look into Ms D's previous relationships and found there was a man called Mr J who died while courting Ms D. The police reinvestigated Mr J's case and found that Ms D poisoned Mr J's food to get his money. Afterwards, the police believed Mr T and arrested Ms D, who is now serving a life sentence.

Lack of Love and Care

Without doubt most marriages that end in divorce are due to lack of love and care between couples. Love and care are two of the essential keys to a healthy and successful matrimony. If spouses do not commit to, love, and care for each other, then their marriage will become unhealthy and unsuccessful. Before two people get married, they always vow to love and care for each other. If they fail to keep their promise, they will struggle to make their relationship work. The purpose of marriage is not just for husbands and wives to live together, but for both to remain truthful and faithful to each other. Couples are supposed to motivate their spouses so that they can bring out the best in them. Spouses are also expected to do things together, to support and perfect each other. Couples must first love their spouse before they can extend their love towards other people. God is love, and anyone that shows love towards another is born of Him.

> *Beloved, let us love one another, for love is of God, and every one who loves is born of God and knows God.*
>
> *—1 John 4:7*

Story 4

Mr and Mrs G have been married for twenty-five years, with two children. According to Mrs G, her husband was selfish and never loved her and their children. She said that the only thing her husband loved and cared about was his job. After a long time at work, her husband would return home stressed and attack her and the children. Her husband's behaviour towards them became worse, and she and the children had to move out of their home.

> *Husbands love your wives and do not be bitter toward them.*
> *—Colossians 3:19*

Story 5

Mr H and Ms J got married and had children together. Ms J was a disciplined mother and a good wife. Unlike Mr H, she never allowed her children to watch violent films or behave immorally. According to Ms J, her husband never cared about her and their children; he was a careless, lazy man who was only interested in watching TV. He complained many times about her not paying attention to him, but she did not take heed to his complaints because he was not a caring and loving spouse. Ms J said her husband was a selfish man who was not ready to be a husband. She divorced him because their marriage was not a caring and loving one.

> *Beloved, if God so loved us, we also ought to love one another.*
> *—1 John 4:11*

> *Owe no one anything except to love one another, for he who loves another has fulfilled the law.*
> *—Romans 13:8*

Many married couples prefer to be in friends' company over their spouse's company. Some women, for example, spend hours with friends talking about the things they experience in their marriage; they do not care to return home early to be with their husband. They behave in this manner because they have lost interest in their husbands and have no affection towards them. Furthermore, some women invite their friends to come and stay overnight or for days, without their husband's approval. When their friends visit and it's time for bed, they allow their husband to go to bed without them because they are busy chatting. A married woman who does not care about her husband will not make him happy and will drive him away.

Men's behaviour is no different from women. Most men prefer to spend more time with friends rather than their wives. Instead of staying at home and talking about the necessary things within their marriage, they would rather hang out elsewhere. Some men go to the pub almost every day, drinking and chatting with pals. If there are things bothering them, instead of talking to their wives first to find a better way to deal with it, they speak to friends and seek advice. They forget that they are married to their wives and not to their friends. Men who behave in such manner have no love for their wives and must learn how to love and care for their wives, who are not just individuals but their flesh.

> *The man said, 'This is now bone of my bones and flesh of my flesh; she shall be called woman, for she was taken out of man.'*
> —*Genesis 2:23*

> *Jesus said to him, 'You shall love the LORD your God with all your heart, with all your soul, and with all your mind.'*
> —*Matthew 22: 37*

> *And the second is like it: 'You shall love your neighbour as yourself.'*
> —*Matthew 22:39*

Religions

Religion is one of the reasons relationships and marriages do not last. Religions' principles and doctrines brainwash individuals, and the spirits that control religions are so wicked that they don't care who they destroy or kill. Religious spirits do have an effect in people's lives, but in different ways. They cause huge problems between husbands and wives.

What is a religion? Religion refers both to the personal practice related to communal faith and to group rituals and communication stemming from shared conviction. It is sometimes used interchangeably with faith or belief system, but it is more socially defined than personal convictions, and it entails specific behaviours. Religion is a belief in a god or gods and the activities connected with this. Religion can involve the worship of numerous things—humans, animals, flowers, goddesses, idols, witchcraft, wizards, unseen beings, mermaid water and objects.

> *You shall have no other gods before Me.*
> *—Exodus 20:3*

> *There shall be no foreign god among you; nor shall you worship any foreign god.*
> *—Psalms 81:9*

> *So you shall not turn aside from any of the words which I command you this day, to the right or the left, to go after other gods to serve them.*
> *—Deuteronomy 28:14*

> *Little children, keep yourselves from idols.*
> *1 John 5:21*

Story 6

One night, I was watching the news. The news was about a young girl killed by her family because she was having a relationship with a Christian boy. She was warned by her Muslim family to stop dating the Christian boy because their religion forbids it. But she refused to end their relationship and kept seeing the Christian boy. Her family was not happy and therefore killed her. The girl would have still been alive if she was not in a relationship with the Christian boy, but unfortunately she died before her time. The father and brothers of the deceased are now serving life sentences. This story shows the extent people can go to destroy lives in the name of religion.

God is real and so are His Words. God is not a man, and neither is He created by men. God is God. He is a Spirit, and He works in truth and in Spirit. Therefore, anybody that worships God must worship Him, in truth and in Spirit. To have a good relationship with God, you must first have a relationship with Jesus Christ. Jesus is the only way to God, and any man or woman who denies the truth about Jesus is not of God. Before you can reach God, you must first go through Jesus. Without Jesus, you are worshiping God in vain. There is only one God, and His name is Jesus—there was none before Him, there is none besides Him, and there will be none after Him.

> 'You are my witness,' says the Lord, 'And My servant whom I have chosen, that you may know and believe Me, and understand that I am He. Before Me there was no God formed, nor shall there be after me.'
>
> —*Isaiah 43:10*

> I, even I, am the Lord, and besides Me there is no Saviour.
>
> —*Isaiah 43:11*

> I am the Alpha and Omega, the Beginning and the End, says the Lord, who is and who was and who is to come, the Almighty.
>
> —*Revelation 1:8*

> I am the Alpha and Omega, the Beginning and the End, the First and the Last.
>
> —*Revelation 22:13*

> I Jesus have sent My angel to testify to you these things in the Churches, I am the root and the offspring of David, and the Bright and Morning Star.
>
> —*Revelation 22:16*

Many people believe that Christianity is a religion. They also believe there is no difference between Christians and other religious worshippers. When I spoke to some Christians about having a relationship with Christ, I found out that some of them are ignorant of the Word of God. They believe that Christianity is a religion and that anyone can have a relationship with God through all religions. I was surprised and shocked that these Christians, who did not know the truth about Christianity, have been attending church since they were infants. However, their lack of knowledge of the truth did not stop me from telling them the truth about Christianity. The Scripture says we shall know the truth and the truth shall make us free (John 8:32).

Religious people are unbelievers—they do not believe in God. Some unbelievers believe in God but live in sin. There are some unbelievers who believe there is a God but refuse to accept that Jesus is the Son of God. Some believe that Jesus is the Son of God but denies that He is God. *Who is a liar but he who denies that Jesus is the Christ? He is antichrist who denies the Father and the Son. Whoever denies the Son does not have the Father either; he who acknowledges the Son has the Father also. (1 John 2:22-23).* Unbelievers adore anything they perceive and do not care if what they are doing is right or wrong. Unbelievers worship human beings, objects, and images that are contrary to the Word of God. Unbelievers adore sinful acts. The Scripture says that Christians must not be in the same level with unbelievers. In spite of what the Scripture says, there are many Christians who embrace sin as the unbelievers.

> *Do not be unequally yoked together with unbelievers. For what fellowship has righteousness with lawlessness? And what communion has light with darkness?*
> —*2 Corinthians 6:14*

Domestic Violence

Domestic violence is another issue that couples experience in their marriage. Domestic violence is used for one purpose only: to gain and maintain total control over a spouse. An abuser does not play fair and uses fear, guilt, shame, and intimidation to wear you down and keep you under their thumb. An abuser may threaten you, hurt you, or hurt those around you.

Intimate relationship violence is the most prevalent form against women. This does not mean that men spouse do not experience violence within marriage, but women spouses are most likely to suffer violence in their matrimonial home than men. Some of these women who experienced such agonising treatment do not remain in marriage; it does not matter what it takes to get out of the marriage, they will do it.

Story 7

Mrs M and her husband had children and lived together for years. During their marital life, Mrs M's husband was violent towards her. As a victim of domestic violence, she searched for help but from the wrong organisations. Mrs M never got the solution to her problems. After many years of enduring domestic violence, she thought the only way she could get out of the violence was to commit suicide.

Story 8

Mr P and Ms K were dating each other and later got engaged. When Ms K moved into Mr P's house, she found out that he was not the good man she thought he was. Mr P did not allow Ms K to install telephone in her bedroom. Mr P erased all her contact numbers from her mobile phone because he did not want her to make contact to anyone. She was restricted from going out, visiting friends, and inviting them to the house. Mr P became very upset with Ms K when he found out that a friend of Ms K's gave her a gift. He was so paranoid that he banged his own head on the wall. He accused Ms K of a lot of things and threatened to strangle her to death if she ever left the house.

Domestic violence could happen to anyone but in different ways. Spouses who reported domestic violence said that their spouses always shout, mock, accuse, call names, and verbally threaten them. Others said that their spouse threatened to withhold money, disconnect the telephone, take the car away, commit suicide, take the children away, and report them to welfare agencies unless they complied with demands regarding bringing up the children. They were persistently put down in front of other people, their money was taken from their purse without their permission, and their telephone calls were interrupted. They also did not receive help with childcare or housework. There are still more undocumented and reported cases where women suffer in their matrimonial home because of domestic violence. Some of these women experienced physical violence such as punching, slapping, biting, pinching, kicking, pulling hair, shoving, burning, and strangling.

In-Laws

While we are happy to have our in-laws in our homes, we do not want them to cause problems between us and our spouse. Our in-laws are part of our lives, and we want them to be there for us—but they should understand that their son or daughter has a new family, and that new family must come first.

Spouses often want one of their relatives to come and stay with them, especially when they start having kids. Sometimes this can cause problems between husbands and wives. For example, you may want your mother to stay in your home looking after your kids; with her help, you do not have to worry about the cost of childcare. Your mother may use this opportunity to overstay, and when your husband complains, you feel he does not like your mother. Due to your inability to take care of your family, your mother wins and your marriage suffers problem.

Some men do allow their mother to live with them and control everything in their home. They sometimes give their mother the right to have her own key to the home, so she can come and go as she pleases. When a mother is given this kind of privilege by her son, the next thing she does is to take charge over her son's family. Some mothers-in-law would not care if their daughter-in-law exists.

Story 9

A woman and her husband have been married for more than eight years with children. She and her husband fight almost all the time because of the husband's mother. Her mother-in-law has a spare key to their home and visits them more than four times each day. According to the woman, one day her mother-in-law entered their home and found them making love. Instead of leaving, she stood in the room for a long period, watching them having sex. The woman said she could not do anything because her mother-in-law controls their home, and if she has complained about her mother-in-law's behaviour, there would have been a serious problem in their marriage.

Sisters-in-law can also cause problems in a marriage. When a woman gets married, she is always excited to move in with one or two of her siblings. They usually prefer their sisters to move in and live with them because they want to be there for them. However, not all women receive good reward for their kindness.

Story 10

Ms A and Mr H were childhood sweethearts. They got married and had seven children. When Ms A's sister moved into their home, she started having an affair with her husband. Ms A was unaware of their iniquity until her husband got her sister pregnant. Ms A was furious and refused to continue living in the same house with her husband. She later filed for divorce.

A marriage of thirty-two years ended because of an ungrateful sister and unfaithful husband. Ms A no longer lives with her husband but her sister does. Her sister has two children with Mr H. When Ms A divorced her husband, she voluntarily permitted her husband to continue committing adultery with her sister. Instead of ending their marriage, Ms A should have rebuilt it. She should have forgiven her husband, and then help him to get marriage counselling.

> *The wise woman builds her house, but the foolish pulls it down with her hands.*
> —*Proverbs 14:1*

The devil is an enemy to success, and one of his evil plans is to make marriages unsuccessful. The devil hates to see married couples live happily ever, and he is doing everything in his power to cause problems between spouses. The devil ends marriages in different ways, and it does not matter to him, who or what he uses to bring an effective matrimony to an end. But whichever way the devil tries to destroy marriages, spouses must not allow it or contribute to what could make their marriage come to an end. Sometimes marriage problems could seem unbearable; however no matter how difficult the problems look, spouses must not give the devil the opportunity to ruin their most beautiful marital life.

F. The Two Important Questions

When a man and woman start dating each other, the two questions predominantly asked by their loved ones are: Does he love you? Is he the right one? It is very important that before the singles say 'I do', they should know if the person they have agreed to marry loves them and is the right one. In chapter one and two, these two questions will be answered to help singles people know when someone loves them and if he/she is the right one.

One

Does He Love You?

I

Does He Love You?

Does he love you? 'Of course he loves me!' How do you know he loves you? 'By the way he looks at me! The way he touches me! The things he says to me!' Sometimes people are roused by the things people say to them; it makes them happy when people say things that they really want to hear. There are people who have sweet tongues and know what to say and how to say it to make a person fall for them. They say things like, 'You are the key of my heart, you are the apple of my eyes, you are the most beautiful woman I have ever met, you are the best thing that has ever happened to me, you are the only woman I have ever loved, I cannot do without you and I cannot live without you.' Some would tell you that they love you more than their mother. They say all these romantic words to you, and yet they will cheat on you, break your heart, put someone else before you, put their business or career before you and some even want you dead before your time.

Sweet tongues are not signs of love, so do not be deceived, because a person that loves you will not break your heart, put someone else before you, put their business or career before you or want you to die before your time. The only way you would know that someone truly loves you is by the way the person treats you, not the things said to you.

> *Love suffers long and is kind; love does not envy; love does not parade itself; is not puffed up.*
>
> —*1 Corinthians 13:4*

A. This Is True Love

God loved us so much that He sent His precious and only Son (Jesus) into this world to save and deliver us. God put us first when He brought His Son into this sinful world to be crucified for our sakes. God is not selfish, and neither has He ever been self-interested. He is a loving, caring, kind and merciful Father. Jesus sacrificed a lot for us; He was rich but for our sakes became poor so that through His poverty we might be rich. If Jesus did not die, many of us would still be living in bondage. The death of Jesus brought full salvation, love, forgiveness, prosperity, freedom, hope and life.

> *For God so loved the world that He gave His only begotten Son, that whoever believes in Him should not perish but have everlasting life.*
>
> *—John 3:16*

> *For God did not send His Son into the world to condemn the world but that the world through Him might be saved.*
>
> *—John 3:17*

> *But God demonstrated his own love towards us, in that while we were sinners, Christ died for us.*
>
> *—Romans 5:8*

> *Greater love has no man than this that a man lay down His life for us.*
>
> *—John 15:13*

> *The thief does not come except to steal, and to kill, and to destroy. I have come that they may have life, and that they may have it more abundantly.*
>
> *—John 10:10*

B. The Man Who Loves You Treats You Well

The man who loves you will respect you. He treats you like a princess and thinks about you all the time. He cares about your happiness and knows when you are not happy and when things are not working fine for you. He does not forget important dates and often buys flowers and cards to show how much he cares and loves you. He is willing to change for you and be a better man. He looks after you when you are feeling down and makes sure you are not left on your own. He knows your favourite foods, songs, books, and movies. He takes you out for lunch and dinner to your favourite restaurants. He loves you so much that he forgives you each time you offend him. The man who loves you puts you first before himself and business. The man who loves you will not plot against you or think about killing you.

Story 1

A boy got his girlfriend pregnant, and when the girl told him about the pregnancy, he was furious and wanted termination. The girl refused to abort the unborn baby, and the boy planned to take her life. His friend (the killer) called the girl to meet up somewhere, and when she arrived, they took her to a nearby river. His friend pushed the girl into the river and held her face underwater to suffocate her. Fortunately she survived. The police were called, and the boys were taken to court for trial. When the judge asked the boyfriend why he wanted to kill her, the boy said it was because of his reputation as a singer. His answer to the judge's question shows that he did not love the girl. The two boys (the singer and his friend) are currently in prison.

C. The Man Who Loves You Communicates and Listens to You

The man who loves you communicates and listens to you at all times. He does not put you off each time you want to talk to him. He understands you and is very thoughtful. He listens to you and considers your opinions. He shares his ideas with you and asks for your thoughts.

He hides nothing from you and always has a good conversation with you. He takes your advice serious as long as it is good advice. He maintains contact with you all the time and enjoys your company. He likes communicating with you, and if he has not heard from you, he will call to know if you are okay.

D. The Man Who Loves You Fellowships with You

The man who loves you fellowships with you! He encourages you to study your Bible when you have not recently read it. He enjoys sharing the Scripture with you. He encourages you to go to church and fellowship with other Christians. He helps you spiritually, and helps maintain your purity in Christ. The man that loves you intercedes for you, prays for you, and prays with you. He evangelises with you. He helps you when you are weak and does not use your weaknesses against you. He encourages you to use your strengths to overcome your weaknesses, through the help of the Holy Spirit.

> *That which we have seen and heard we declare to you, that you also may have fellowship with us; and truly our fellowship is with the Father and with His Son Jesus Christ.*
>
> —*1 John 1:3*

> *I urge you first of all, to pray for all people. Ask God to help them; intercede on their behalf, and give thanks for them.*
>
> —*1 Timothy 2:1*

> *Likewise the Holy Spirit also helps in our weaknesses. For we do not know what we should pray for as we ought, but the Holy Spirit Himself makes intercession for us with groaning which cannot be uttered.*
>
> —*Roman 8:26*

E. The Man Who Loves You Does Not Make You Feel Unhappy

The man who loves you does not make you feel unhappy and uncomfortable. He does not compare you to anyone else. He is not ashamed of you, and neither is he ashamed to introduce you to his family and friends. He does not belittle you in front of his friends or family. He does not make you feel bad about yourself. He loves you because of whose you are, not because of what you have. He does not force you to sleep with him to prove how much you love him. He does not stare at women to make you jealous. The man who loves you does not seduce you or make you feel dejected because you refused to sleep with him.

Story 2

A born-again and worker in a church seduced a sister. They had known each other for a long time but were not in a relationship. The man believed that the sister was the one for him, yet he was afraid of commitment. He called the sister on the phone once in a blue moon. One day, he visited the sister and was very upset because he was in a sticky situation. When the sister started to console him, he took advantage of her. He seduced the sister, forced himself on top of her, and then started kissing her body. The sister pushed him away and told him to leave her house. He turned and said to the sister, 'You are not romantically moved.' This kind of behaviour is immoral, and the brother did not show that he had the image of Christ. No wonder—the Scripture says by their fruits we shall know them.

> *Beware of false prophets, who come to you in sheep's clothing, but inwardly they are ravenous wolves.*
> —*Matthew 7:15*

> *You will know them by their fruits. Do men gather grapes from thorn-bushes or figs from thistles?*
> —*Matthew 7:16*

F. The Man Who Loves You Does Not Leave You for Someone Else

The man who truly loves you will not leave you for another woman. He stays with you when others reject you. He sees you as a nice person and is not ashamed of you. He is proud of you and proud to be your friend. He looks after you when no one else does. He remains with you and never deserts you when things are going poorly. He makes you see that your tomorrow will always be better than your yesterday. The man who loves you sees you as irreplaceable. When you are ill, he takes good care of you, making sure that you get better by providing the things you need to recover. The man who loves you sees you as his number one. He does not see you as second class or treat you in a manner that makes you feel inferior. The man who loves you will not cause you grief or sorrow. He will not harm you or allow anything that will bring destruction to your life.

Story 3

There was a beauty queen who had everything going for her. When she won the contest, she was signed for a lot of contracts to appear in magazines. Her popularity and reputation brought a man into her life who couldn't think about anything else other than her. She started dating this man and later got engaged to him. One thing she did not know was that her fiancé was in love with someone else. When she found out that her fiancé was about to marry another woman, she was fuming, and she had no option but to leave him. The day she was removing all her belongings from her fiancé's house, she slipped, fell from the balcony, and died.

Story 4

Ms N, a born-again Christian, followed a friend home to spend time with her. Ms N was loved by everyone because of her moral behaviour. Whilst she was staying with her friend, she met Mr G, an unbeliever and a rich business man. Mr G was the general manager of the company owned by Ms N's friend's husband. When

Mr G met Ms N, he fell for her and gave her the impression that she was the one for him. They started going out and convinced everyone they were madly in love. The way things were between them, everyone thought that their relationship was the kind that ends in marriage. No one imagined that Mr G was playing Ms N—until their relationship ended. Mr G had another woman in mind; a woman he knew and adored before he met Ms N. Ms N was devastated and heartbroken when Mr G left her for another woman. She thought that Mr G was genuinely in love with her and that one day she could become Mrs G.

Story 5

A university boy met a girl. He loved the girl so much that he rented a flat for the two of them and paid all the bills and utilities. He was interested in marrying the girl but had no clue that the girl had her eyes on someone else. When he found out that the girl he had been living and sharing everything together was getting married to another man, he became so very angry and depressed that he made a regrettable decision. He rejoined his former gang (which he had previously left because the things they did were evil). He thought that going back to his former gang and doing those things would help him forget the girl and what she did to him. Whilst with the gang at night, they saw the police and started to run. The police ran after them, and the boy was shot and he died at the spot. The boy wanted to be a better person when he left his former gang, and he looked forward to the future. He truly thought he had found a true love. He was ready to start a new life and family with the girl. He had a bright future and planned to become a born-again, but all of it was taken away from him.

Two

Is He the Right One?

II

Is He the Right One?

People always think that the person they fall for is the right one for them. If they were right, many marriages would not have ended in divorce. It might be easy for some people to fall in love or find someone to love; however, finding that one chosen by God is not that easy. The Holy Spirit is the only one who can connect people to the right spouse. It is imperative that people give their life to Christ so that they can receive the Holy Spirit.

> *So then, those who are in the flesh cannot please God.*
> *—Roman 8:8*

> *But you are not in the flesh but in the Spirit, if indeed the Spirit of God dwells in you. Now if anyone does not have the Spirit of Christ, he is not His.*
> *—Roman 8:9*

A. The Right One Is Chosen by God

When God created Adam, he formed Eve to be his wife because he knew she would be right for him. God is the creator of every man and woman; He knew us before we were born, and He knows the right spouse for each of us. Many people pick the wrong spouse, not just because they are unbelievers but because they do not trust God enough to allow Him to choose the right person for them. God works with time and He knows the best time to confirm who He has chosen for you as a spouse.

B. The Right One Is the Bone of Your Bones and the Flesh of Your Flesh

The right one is that person that has something in common with you, that shares your values and interests. The right one sees you like his flesh and blood and loves you in the manner he loves himself. The right one is not insecure when he is around you. The right one treats you like a diamond because he knows you are a very special person. The right one hurts when you are hurting. When you are sad, he is sad; when you are happy, he is happy. The right one understands you more than anyone else. The right one knows when something is bothering or worrying you, and when you are not happy about something, he does his best to make you feel all right.

> *This is now bone of my bones and flesh of my flesh; she shall be called Woman because she was taken out of Man.*
>
> —*Genesis 2:23*

> *Therefore a man shall leave his father and mother and be joined to his wife, and they shall become one flesh.*
>
> —*Genesis 2:24*

C. The Right One Is Not Afraid of Commitment

The right one is never confused, and he is not afraid to face the future. The right one would first want to know you better before taking your relationship further, to marriage. He is husband material and knows what it takes to be a better man and the best husband. He understands the importance of marriage and having a family. The right one will not cheat on you or play you. He does not use you to get want he wants. The right one is not afraid of commitment and is ready to commit to a long-lasting relationship.

> *The Lord, He is the One who goes before you. He will be with you; He will not leave you nor forsake you; do not fear nor be dismayed.*
>
> —*Deuteronomy 31:8*

Fear not, for I am with you; be not dismayed, for I am your
God. I will strengthen you, yes, I will help you, I will uphold
you with My righteous right hand.

Isaiah 41:10

D. The Right One Knows Your Dos and Don'ts

The right one knows your dos and don'ts. He will not lie to you. The right one will not do things that will annoy you. The right one will not force or make you to do things you don't like. He will not criticise you or make you feel bad when you are not doing things he wants you to do. The right one will never beat you. The right one will not hurt or injure you. The right one is that person that does not sexually abuse you. The right one does his best to put things right when things are not going well. The right one is that person respects your gut feelings and emotions. The right one is that person that respects you for who you really are.

E. The Right One Knows His Image

The right one knows he is the image of Christ. The right one is not ashamed of who he represents. He does not try to be whom he is not to please you. He does not copy from people, but he learns. The right one is born of God, and he puts God first before everything he does. The right one is the one that takes you to church, not the one you force to go to church with you. The right one loves the presence of God, and enjoys fellowshipping with children of God. The right one is not an idol worshipper, and neither is he religious. The right one does not cover his sins. He is not over righteous. The right one is that person that does not nail Jesus on the cross but matches the true image of Him.

He who covers his sins will not prosper, but whoever confesses
and forsakes them will have mercy.

—Proverbs 28:13

Do not be overly righteous, nor be overly wise: Why should you destroy yourself?

—*Ecclesiastes 7:16*

For whom He foreknew, He also predestined to be conformed to the image of His Son.

—*Romans 8:29*

F. The Right One Is Very Supportive

The right one supports you spiritually, mentally, and physically. The right one is that person that shares the Word of God with you. He encourages you to read your Bible at all times, and ensures you do not backslide. The right one is that person that supports you in everything you do, as long as it is the will of God. The right one is that person that helps with your studies if you are a student. The right one is that person that supports you in your business and always come up with ideas that will help you to excel. He eases your burden of work. He prays for your success and celebrates with you when it happens.

G. The Right One Is Cultivated

Many people are not cultivated. God designed human beings to be cultivators and will never give them a finished man or woman. A lot of people do not know the purpose of God for their lives. They are only just surviving, merely living for living sake. They do not have challenging goals or serious ambition, and are comfortable settling with average. God did not create us to settle with average or remain in the same position. God's desires are for His children to prosper from one position to another. Grow, develop and elevate in everything they do. Christians are created to be leaders. Therefore, they should be the head and not the tail.

Beloved, I pray that you may prosper in all things and be in health, just as your soul prospers.

—*3 John 1:2*

The righteous shall flourish like a palm tree; he shall grow like a cedar in Lebanon.

—Psalms 92:12

And the LORD will make you the head and not the tail; you shall be above only, and not be beneath, if you heed the commandments of the LORD your God, which I command you today, and are careful to observe them.

—Deuteronomy 28:13

H. The Right One Does Not Reject You

The right one is always there when you are sick or not able to look after yourself. The right one stands by you when no one wants you. The right one sees you as his best friend and will not take you for granted. When you are lonely, he helps you beat the spirit of loneliness. When you think that all hope is gone, he will remind you of what the Word of God says concerning your life. He will make you see sense and help you overcome the difficulties and challenges of life. The right one is that person that will not leave or forsake you when things get tougher. The right one is unique, one in a million.

I. The Right One Does Not Judge You

The right one does not condemn you, and neither does he criticize you. If he is not happy about something, he talks to you gently about it with love, dignity, and respect. The right one will always defend you when people say bad things about you. He is that person that cautions you with love, and he corrects you when you have done something wrong. The right one is that person that does not say bad things about you behind your back. He does not make your life worse when you are not in your best. The right one is that person that admires and appreciates your life as a Christian and encourages you to pray without ceaseless. The right one is that person that encourages you to spend more time with God than man. He does not judge you but helps bring out the best in you.

Judge not, that you be not judged.

—Matthew 7:1

For with what judgment you judge, you will be judged; and with the measure you use, it will be measured back to you.

—Matthew 7:2

Why do you look at the speck in your brother's eye, but do not consider the plank in your own eye?

—Matthew 7:3

Or how can you say to your brother, 'Let me remove the speck from your eye'; and look, a plank is in your own eye?

—Matthew 7:4

Hypocrites! First remove the plank from your own eye, and then you will see clearly to remove the speck from your brother's eye.

—Matthew 7:5

J. The Right One Is Always There When You Need Him

The right one is that person that is always there, when you are in need. No matter what your situation is, he will always love and cherish you. The right one is that person that appreciates each moment he spends with you. He gives you more attention than anybody else, and he does not see you as a burden. The right one is indeed a special friend, which not many people possess. The right one is warm and tender and comforting in his care. The right one is there for you willingly and comes freely; he is never bought. He listens and really hears what you have to say. The right one is that person that is reliable and in him you can confide. The right one greets you with open arms and love. He feels your presence whether near or far. The right one is that one that is prudent and a blessing from God.

Houses and riches are an inheritance from fathers, but a prudent wife is from the Lord.

—Proverbs 19:14

K. The Right One Sticks Closer

When you are in serious trouble, make a huge mistake, are extremely depressed, or are short of money, the right one will be more than happy to help you in these types of situation, without reservation. He will not spread your gossip to other people and will be there to offer advice and support. The right one is the friend you trust 100 per cent. The right one will pick you when you are down and will be a shoulder to cry when you are upset. He will make time for you when you are in need of his company. The right one will share your good and bad news. The right one is interested in all aspects of your life. The right one is that person that does not leave you because of what people say about you. The right one is a true friend, and he sticks closer than a brother.

> *A man who has friends must himself be friendly, but there is a friend who sticks closer than a brother.*
> —*Proverbs 18:24*

L. The Right One Sees Marriage as an Honour

The right one sees marriage as a credit and understands the true meaning of marriage. The right one knows that marriage is a commitment, and prepares himself as a future husband. He does not think about the single life and hanging out with mates, or what he would miss if becomes a husband. He thinks about getting married and having a family of his own. The right one is that person that is not interested in your money or property or family assets. The right one is only interested in you because he loves you and wants to spend the rest of his life with you. He does not mess around or sleep around. The right one sees marriage as an honour and respects the bed of purity.

> *Marriage is honourable among all, and the bed undefiled; but fornicators and adulterers God will judge.*
> —*Hebrews 13:4*

Three

Love at First Sight

III

Love at First Sight

Love at first sight is an emotional condition whereby a person feels a romantic or sexual attraction for a stranger during the first encounter. Love at first sight is just sex and ego. It is also described as being lust.

Lust is defined as 'desire for what is forbidden; an obsessive craving.' Lust is a strong, sexual desire you have for somebody, for things that are contrary to the will of God. It is also defined as not simply desire but illegitimate, unlawful, illicit, or forbidden desire.

> *Do not love the world or the things in the world. If anyone loves the world, the love of the Father is not in him.*
> —1 John 2:15

> *For all that is in the world, the lust of the flesh, the lust of the eyes, and the pride of life, is not of the Father but is of the world.*
> —1 John 2:16

Story 1

The first time Mr and Mrs G met, they were crazy about each other. Mrs G was a university student at the time and was described by Mr G as a very beautiful, intelligent girl. Mr G could not resist Mrs G's beauty and proposed to her six weeks after they met. They got married, and Mrs G got pregnant shortly thereafter but refused to carry the baby. This was not due to medical reasons but because she was fretted that her pregnancy would show during her university graduation ceremony. Mr G was devastated when his wife terminated their unborn child, and he later filed for divorce.

Mr and Mrs G's story is heartbreaking. Two people who hardly knew each other thought they were in love, and they rushed into marriage within weeks. This was not love but lust of the flesh. It was Mrs G's outward beauty that lured Mr G into marriage. They were never in love and did not understand the true meaning of love. If the love they both had for each other were genuine, then Mrs G would not have terminated their unborn baby, and Mr G would not have divorced her.

> *Do not lust after her beauty in your heart, nor let her allure you with her eyelids.*
>
> —*Proverbs 6:25*

Those who are lured into a relationship because of a person's sexual appearance do not always have a long-lasting relationship. Though it might be sweet at the beginning, the end destroys the soul. During the time of my discourse with people about relationships, I discovered that some women prefer to marry tall, handsome, and built men. The men said they prefer to marry women who are tall and pretty with a curvy figure. It was a shock that none of the people I spoke to desired to marry a God-fearing man or a virtuous woman. What men consider as beauty is not what God regards as beauty. This was the reason God said to Samuel not to look at the man's physical appearance *(But the Lord said to Samuel, "Do not look at his appearance or at his physical stature, because I have refused him. For the Lord does not see as man sees, for man looks at the outward appearance, but the Lord looks at the heart." (1 Samuel 16:7)*. The beauty of a man is not his personal looks but his mind or spirit. When you desire the outward beauty of a person, you are walking in the flesh and not in the Spirit. But when you walk in the Spirit, you will not fulfil the lust of the flesh.

> *I say then: Walk in the Spirit, and you shall not fulfil the lust of the flesh.*
>
> —*Galatians 5:16*

Story 2

There was a man called Mr Casanova because he lusted for beautiful women. Each night he returned home with different kinds of women. Everyone at the neighbourhood knew about his addiction to beautiful women. One evening, Mr Casanova returned from work with a beautiful lady. She was light in complexion and was tall. Mr Casanova refused to drop her off at home the next day because he genuinely liked her. He was crazy about her and admitted that their relationship was not a one night stand. He longed for a serious relationship that would lead to marriage.

One night they were asleep. He opened his eyes and noticed there was a strange object beside him. When he turned, he saw a long snake lying next to him. He screamed, and the snake crawled and disappeared. The snake was the lady. Mr Casanova became so afraid that he gave his life to Jesus shortly after his terrifying experience.

> *But each one is tempted when he is carried away and enticed by his own lust.*
> *—James 1:14*

> *Then when lust has conceived, it gives birth to sin; and when sin is accomplished, it brings forth death.*
> *—James 1:15*

> *There is a way which sees right unto a man but the end thereof is the ways of death.*
> *—Proverbs 14:12*

> *A man's steps are of the Lord; how then can a man understand his own way?*
> *—Proverbs 20:24*

> *But I say to you that whoever looks at a woman to lust for her has already committed adultery with her in his heart.*
> *—Matthew 5:28*

If we confess our sins, He is faithful and just to forgive us our sins, and cleanse us from all unrighteousness.

—*1 John 1:9*

But as many as received Him, to them He gave the right to become children of God, to those who believe in His name.

—*John 1:12*

What would you have done if you were Mr Casanova? Would you have given your life to Christ as Mr Casanova did? Mr Casanova was lucky and should thank God that the snake did not strangle him. The Scripture says that the devil is like a roaring lion seeking whom to devour ('*Be sober, be vigilant, because your adversary the devil walks about like a lion, seeking whom he may devour*'—*1 Peter 5:8*). Satan might not come in the form of a lion, but he comes in the form of human beings to destroy those who are obsesses with women and are weak like Mr Casanova. If Mr Casanova had not opened his eyes that night, he would not have known that the lady was a serpent. If their relationship had ended in marriage, Mr Casanova would have been married to Lucifer.

There are many people living life like Mr Casanova, and they are not aware of what their sinful behaviour could attract in the future. There are both female and male serpents brought into the world by the devil to seduce people. It is hard to tell who is not and who is from the devil. Some of them are in churches today, working and pretending to be one of the followers of Christ. They do not have to change into a serpent, but they have the spirit of serpent controlling them. Sometimes when spouses experience problems in their marriage, it is caused by serpent spirits. This is why it is important to be a born-again Christian and worship in a true Bible-preached ministry.

What happened to Mr Casanova could happen to anyone. Mr Casanova survived, but you may not be as lucky. This serpent men and women are on a mission, and the mission must be completed for the devil to have victory. The devil is targeting marriages, and he is doing everything in his power to obliterate them. He is attracting and connecting people to wrong spouses; this is one of the easiest ways he could ruin marriages. Furthermore, the devil manipulates the married and turns their minds away from their spouses. The spouses, who are controlled by the serpent spirits, wouldn't know what they are doing until that strange man or woman causes problems between them and their spouse.

A lot of people are like Mr Casanova and wait for the bad to happen before they can change from their immoral behaviour. No one should experience what Mr Casanova experienced. The whole time Mr Casanova was eating and sleeping with the lady, he never knew he was sleeping with the devil. If Mr Casanova was a born-again, he would have noticed a strange behaviour around him. He was unable to perceive spiritually because he was a sinner living an ungodly life. God speaks to His children every day, and they hear Him. But Mr Casanova was not a child of God and therefore could not hear from Him.

Brethrens! Do not be wise; fear the Lord and depart from evil. The Lord is at your door knocking, and whoever opens for Him, He dines with him. When a person begins to have a good relationship with the Lord, the person will no longer live in the flesh but in the spirit. If he prays to God, He answers him because he is no longer a transgressor. But when a sinner prays to God, his prayers are belated because his sin has separated him from God.

> _Do not be wise in your own eyes; Fear the Lord and depart from evil._
> > —_Proverbs 3:7_

> _Behold, I stand at the door and knock. If anyone hears My voice and opens the door, I will come in to him and dine with him, and he with Me._
> > —_Revelation 3:20_

> _Behold the Lords hand is not shortened, that it cannot save; nor His ear heavy, that it cannot hear._
> > —_Isaiah 59:1_

> *But your iniquities have separated between you and God, and*
> *your sins have hid his face from you that he will not hear.*
> *—Isaiah 59:2*

A. COUNSEL

Christians are expected to change their hearts for God and unremittingly make great effort to live for Him. If Christians change their hearts for the world, they desire the things which the world offers, and that is the time they are guilty of the "lust of the flesh and the lust of the eyes". The "lust of the eyes" obviously refers to what is seen, what the world wants to see. The eyes enjoy things of beauty, and when the world lusts after those things, it is the lust of eyes. To lust for a man or a woman is a sin. To make someone desire you is a sin, and if you admire someone sexually, you have committed adultery within your heart.

> *But I say to you that whoever looks at a woman to lust for her*
> *has already committed adultery with her in his heart.*
> *—Matthew 5:28*

Do not let a person's superficial beauty lure you to marriage. Marriage is a commitment. You do not want to marry someone, and then tomorrow the marriage is over. When you are selecting a spouse, do not choose a person because of outward beauty. Choose a person who is husband or wife material, who has a good moral personality. Furthermore, if you meet someone and are interested in him/her, try to find out more about that person. Find out about the person's character, belief, family, background, lifestyle, and what he or she does for a living.

We all need God to direct us in everything we do, and that includes directions to find the right spouse. Those who put God first in everything they do and those who do the will of God live forever.

> *The world is passing away, and also its lusts; but the one who*
> *does the Will of God lives forever.*
> *—1 John 2:17*

Four

Lack of Communication

IV

Lack of Communication

Communication is the process of transferring information from one person to another; it is the act of sharing or exchanging information, ideas, or feelings. The question is: how important is communication? The simple answer is that communication is very important in our daily lives because if people do not communicate, they will not get what they need in life. When people cannot get what they need in life, they are unable to succeed. Communication is so important that a person has to be a good communicator before he/she can work well with others. Communication is also very important in relationships and marriages. Spouses who do not communicate well with their spouse do not always have a healthy relationship. Good communication is one of the keys to a successful marriage, and a lack of communication is the first step towards an unsuccessful one.

The beginning of a lack of communication between husband and wife is usually the inability to talk about little things, which turn into bigger things when frustration and anger are built up. It is necessary that spouses have time for each other to talk about issues that trouble them within the marriage, and be able to solve them without struggle and argument.

When spouses communicate effectively, it shows they have respect for each other. Spouses do not have to be talkative to be able to communicate with their spouse. Although there are quiet spouses, it is still important that they converse with their other half. The communication does not need to be by means of words alone; simple acts of patting, caressing, or holding hands are a great form of communication. They dissolve resentments over perceived or actual slights, bridge distances, and generate positive energy.

Story 1

Mr H and his wife have a young daughter. Mr H does not like spending time with his wife and daughter and prefers to spend most of his time on his computer. His lack of communication is causing his wife to feel alone and lonely. Sometimes they do not speak to each other for days, and their marriage is suffering. Each time they make love, they do not feel the passion, and as a result they end up not satisfying each other.

> *Let the husband render to his wife the affection due her, and likewise also the wife to her husband.*
> —*1 Corinthians 7:3*

In a marriage where communication is the main key, there is also good listening aptitude. Spouses who communicate well with each other are good listeners too. Being a good listener shows how much the love and care about each other; it shows that spouses can have confidence in their spouse when sharing their feelings and ideas. Problems can develop if husband and wife do not pay attention to what the other is saying. However, if they learn how to focus and concentrate when the other is talking, they will be able develop a good listening ability.

Husbands who do not communicate with their wives are those that consider their wives inferior; this rarely, if ever, makes for a good relationship. The same is true of wives; if they look down upon their husbands, then they can never hope to gain their confidence and affection. When a husband and wife discuss uncomfortable issues, it helps build a good relationship. Sometimes it is hard for spouses to discuss with their spouse about things they have done wrong; it requires great courage to admit faults. But if their spouse is a caring and loving person and will stand by them, then they have nothing to worry about. What they need to do is to feel free to discuss those subjects that they see as a burden, so that the emotional bonds between them and their spouse will become much stronger.

Empathy is one more way of communicating; it is the capability to understand another person's emotion and feelings. It is often characterised as the ability to put oneself into another's shoes. It does not necessarily imply compassion, sympathy, or empathic concern because this capacity can be present in context of compassionate or cruel behaviour. Empathy is the unspoken communication. A spouse must show concern when things go wrong. A husband and wife do not have to express it; the mere body language becomes a source of comfort. It makes you feel stronger if your spouse holds your hand and says that you can overcome your trials and tribulations. All of a sudden, you do not feel alone, and the marriage grows deeper.

Lack of communication in relationship can result in rapid decisions and lead to separation. Spouses need to know the reasons behind communication failure and how they can be corrected, so that they can have a successful marriage. But what causes communication failure between spouses?

Communication failure between spouses can occur when one person changes and grows but the other one does not. As much as couples would like to capture time and freeze it during the honeymoon phase, the reality is that outside forces shape their lives. Many times people go into marriage thinking that their spouse will stay exactly the same. While it is easy to notice a change in a spouse, if the change occurs to oneself it is not so easy to recognise it.

Communication failure between spouses occurs when one spouse cannot make the other understand how they feel. This can be due to one person not listening, or the other person not talking about how they feel. Perhaps both spouses have different ways of communicating, but their spouse does not understand what they are trying to say.

Communicate failure between spouses can occur as a result of moving to a new place or area, finding a new job, making new friends, having a new baby. For example, when the first baby arrives, the mother has to give more time to the baby, and the father often has to spend more time at work. Consequently they get few chances to talk, and when that happens; there are complaints and disagreements over inconsequential issues. Sometimes the argument could be the needs of the child, and how it should be handled and cared for. If the argument becomes uncontrollable, they will end their communication and become reserved. If both spouses realised that they have ceased to communicate well, then this issue can be resolved. It is harder to keep communication and the marriage going if only one spouse recognises the need for it.

Communication failure between spouses is sometimes caused by stress at work, which makes the person to withdraw and get easily annoyed. If the person tries to resolve issues, the argument results in more problems, and eventually he/she stops discussing things, no matter what the problem is. The person may not want to discuss anything with their spouse and start hiding problems. Spouses might be afraid that if they open up, they would annoy their loved one even more, and therefore they chose not to disclose to each other.

Communication failure between spouses can occur when spouses do not trust each other, especially when there are doubts about the other's faithfulness. For instance, some spouses observe their spouse's actions and make no effort to discuss their doubts with them. But when the third party gets involve, they are willing to open up to that third party instead of discussing things between themselves. It is best for spouses to resolve their problems by themselves than to rely on a third party.

Communication failure between spouses usually occurs when spouses live far apart from each other. If your spouse lives far from you, ensure you communicate on a regular basis and never let distance come in the way of your love. When spouses live apart, their relationship will be hard to manage, but if they make a decision not to let distant ruin it and stick to that decision, their marriage will remain unbroken.

Lack of communication is a big issue in marriage. If spouses do not communicate with each other, they will know nothing about them. However, if spouses communicate well, they will be surprised at what they can learn. They will be aware of the things that can cause problems in their marriage, and they may be better equipped to recognise when those problems occur and can deal with them efficiently.

Story 2

One evening I was watching the news, and some men were asked about how much they knew about their wives. Some of the questions they were asked include their wives' dress, shoe size, and favourite perfumes. To my surprise, the men gave wrong answers. This shows that a lot married men do not know much about their wives. After watching the programme, I asked myself what would make a husband not to know his wife and the things she likes. The answer that came in my mind was a lack of communication.

A. COUNSEL

It is reasonable to find out why you and your spouse are having a hard time communicating. There could be many reasons why you cannot converse—you and your spouse do not have enough time to talk, you are concerned that your spouse is not the understandable type, you are afraid of a potential argument that may arise. Whatever the reasons may be, you must identify what holds you back from communicating actively and openly, because this is the first step to making progress.

Good communication is one of the main keys to a successful marriage, and it can be done in several ways. For instance, you can communicate face to face, or by telephone, mobile, text message, e-mail, or letter writing. If you do not communicate to your spouse, he will not know your mind. When you communicate verbally to your spouse, ensure you speak with a soft tone of voice; this will help smooth the conversation.

When you feel that your other half will not communicate verbally for whatever reasons, try not to be troubled; you can communicate to him/her by e-mail. Using e-mail will help you voice the things that you would not want to discuss with your spouse in person. Though not everyone has the confidence to use e-mail, there are other alternatives, such as text messages and letter writing.

You can start communicating little by little through text messages. Although text boxes have word limit, this is not a problem because you're not expected to discuss everything in this manner. Your text messages should include words like those you used while on honeymoon, those that inspired your spouse during the time you were dating.

Letter writing is another way to communicate to your spouse. Communicating through letter writing is very useful because it gives you the chance to say everything that is in your mind. With letter writing you do not have to worry about word limit. However, write clearly and avoid using abusive words (no matter how angry you are with your spouse).

If you do not spend time together with your spouse, the connection you have fades. You and your spouse should try to talk to each other and know what is in each other's minds. Reasons behind lack of communication vary from couple to couple, but the important thing is that you should not let these problems come in the way of your relationship. You should always talk things out between yourselves, before they get worse, and never let lack of communication lead to misunderstandings and distrust in your relationship.

It is not good to always discuss serious themes with your spouse at ever conversation, because this could spoil communication when you both find yourselves dreading discussions or being around one another. If you go back to when you and your spouse were dating, you will remember there were topics you enjoyed discussing; try to talk about them again because it will help things between the two of you. You should talk for the sake of talking to each other. You should swap stories with each other about childhoods, jobs experience, interest, and hobbies. This will also help to maintain the feeling of friendship in your marriage, which is absolutely essential to maintain good communication.

One more way to build up a good relationship is to discuss awkward subjects. It is very hard to tell your spouse that your manager mistreated you or that you made a fool of yourself before your colleagues at work. It is true that it requires great courage to own up your faults, but if you have a caring spouse, and if you believe that your other half will stand by you, then you must discuss issues that hurt your pride. By doing so, you will find that you have lifted a big mental burden. More than that, the emotional bonds between you and your spouse will become stronger.

Good communication is a vital instrument to a successful marriage. To communicate effectively in marriage, spouses must know how to communicate well. The main requirement to have good communication within marriage is to respect each other. People who belittle their spouses hardly make their relationship to work. If they look down on their spouses, then they can never gain their assurance and affection.

Five

Alcohol

V

Alcohol

Alcohol is a drug that has the immediate effect of altering one's mood. Many people think drinking it makes them feel energetic, happy, and even euphoric—but in fact alcohol is a depressant that switches off the part of the brain that controls judgement, leading to a loss of inhibitions. Drinking even small amounts of alcohol can affect physical coordination. Alcohol can be a fast or slow poison. It slows the brain's activities and the activity of the spinal cord. Consumed over many years, it may cause damage to the body; consumed in higher quantities than the body is unable to cope with, it may cause sudden death.

When a person drinks alcohol, about 20 per cent is absorbed in the stomach, and 80 per cent is absorbed in the small intestine. The concentration of alcohol, the type of drink, and whether the stomach is full or empty depends on how fast the alcohol is absorbed. Once the alcohol is absorbed into the tissue, it affects the person's mind and body. Blood alcohol concentration can rise up to twenty minutes after having a drink. After alcohol is absorbed, it leaves (and damages) the body in five ways—the brain, heart, kidneys, lungs, and liver.

Alcohol is not good for both the young and old. Alcohol is a silent killer that has destroyed many lives and marriages. Yet many people say they drink it to forget their misery and worries. I came across a man who was having a bad time, and he was drinking alcohol. I spoke to him concerning his drinking, and he said to me that he drinks because it helps him to forget his sorrows. There is no doubt that alcohol makes people forget themselves for some hours after consuming it. However, it does not solve the problems for them. A person who has a problem and thinks that drinking alcohol is the solution is making a big mistake, because consuming alcohol will not solve the problem—rather it will make it worse. As a result, the person's sorrow or misery will become too much for them to bear.

> *Who has woe? Who has sorrow? Who has contentions? Who has complaints? Who has wounds without cause? Who has redness of eyes?*
>
> —*Proverbs 23:29*

> *Those who linger long at the wine, those who go in search of mixed wine.*
>
> —*Proverbs 23:30*

> *Do not look on the wine when it is red, when it sparkles in the cup, when it swirls around smoothly.*
>
> —*Proverbs 23:31*

> *At the last it bites like a serpent, and stings like a viper.*
>
> —*Proverbs 23:32*

The Scripture says, 'Give strong drink to him who is ready to perish, and wine to those who are heavy hearted. Let him drink, and forget his poverty, and remember his misery no more' (Proverbs 31:6-7). These two verses confuse a lot of people because many believe that the Scripture says they can drink alcohol when they are in difficulties or passing through rough times. What the Scripture is trying to tell us is that people who drink alcohol are those who think all hope is gone and those who are prepared to die. The Scripture gave us two choices: to live or die. It is up to us to choose whether to do something about our difficulty and live, or choose to drink alcohol (the destroyer) and die, so that we don't have to worry about our misery anymore. The choice is in our hands.

God's purpose for us is to enjoy and live life to the fullest. God does not want His children to perish, and neither does He encourage them to drink anything that will bring their lives to an end. What the Almighty God wants from us is to pray about the things troubling our lives and marriage. He wants us to commit our troubles and sorrows into His hands. His will for man is to have faith in Christ, because He alone can bring solution to man's misery and sorrow. Furthermore, kings and princes are not expected to drink alcohol. Christians are the kings and princes—therefore Christians must not drink or eat anything unclean.

> *It is not for kings, to drink wine, nor for princes to drink strong drink.*
> —*Proverbs 31:4*

> *Now therefore, please be careful not to drink wine or similar drink, and not to eat anything unclean.*
> —*Judges 13:4*

Story 1

Mr O was a married man with two children. He was a nice man but changed when he started consuming alcohol. Each time he drinks alcohol; he urinates inside his trousers and says things that were very offensive. He was belittled, scorned, and laughed at by both children and adults. The colour of his eyes changed to red because of his binge drinking. His wife and children left him because they could not put up with his drinking and shameful behaviour.

> *Wine is a mocker, Strong drink is a brawler, and whoever is led astray by it is not wise.*
> —*Proverbs 20:1*

Story 2

Ms S and her husband have been married for years. Before they got married, Mr S was not an alcoholic. According to Ms S, her husband was a man who did not listen or take advice from people. Ms S described her husband as a man without a good behaviour, and he sometimes acted uncouthly. Her husband's bad behaviour became worse when he began to drink alcohol. He started to drink alcohol because he was made redundant. Each time he drank, he argued with Ms S. When Ms S could not put up with his drinking, she finally left him.

The Word of God is what people need when they are made redundant. People who drink alcohol because they lost their jobs are adding more problems to their lives. Alcohol does not help anyone—it makes things worse. The Word of God gives hope, and those who believe in it overcome their problems. The Word of God is written to help us in times of need, so that we know that God never fails. The Word of God is written for us to know that we are not alone, when we are down or heavy-hearted. The Word of God is powerful and is the only solution to our problems. What a Christian needs to do in time of redundancy or trouble is to call God.

> *He shall call upon Me, and I will answer him; I will be with him in trouble; I will deliver him and honour him.*
> —*Psalms 91:15*

> *Call to Me, and I will answer you, and show you great and mighty things, which you do not know.*
> —*Jeremiah 33:3*

> *Come to Me, all you who labour and are heavy laden and I will give you rest.*
> —*Matthew 11:28*

> *Take My yoke upon you and learn from Me, for I am gentle and lowly in heart, and you will find rest for your souls.*
> —*Matthew 11:29*

> *He heals the broken hearted, and binds up their wounds.*
> —*Psalms 147:3*

Another verse in the Scripture concerning alcohol that confuses many people is where Jesus turned water into wine (John 2:7-8). The question many Christians have asked is: 'If alcohol is not good, why did Jesus turn water into wine'. There is nothing wrong with asking questions, especially when a person does not understand something. However, it is wrong to ask an incorrect question. Those confused should have asked what kind of wine the Scripture is talking about—whether it is the wine made with fruits but alcoholic free, or whether it is the wine that contains alcohol. The wine Jesus made from water was a supernatural wine, and no one has ever produced such a wine. Although the Scripture did not expressly state the type of wine it was, neither did it say that the wine contained alcohol. Therefore, no one should assume that the wine which Jesus made was alcoholic, or else they will be fallaciously adding their own words.

> *Whatever I command you, be careful to observe it; you shall not add to it nor take away from it.*
> —*Deuteronomy 12:32*

> *Do not add to His words, lest He rebuke you, and you be found a liar.*
> —*Proverbs 30:6*

> *For I testify to everyone who hears the Words of the prophecy of this book: If anyone adds to these things, God will add to him the plagues that are written in this book.*
> —*Revelation 22:18*

> *If anyone takes away from the Words of the book of this prophecy, God shall take away his part from the Book of Life, from the holy city, and from the things which are written in this book.*
> —*Revelation 22:19*

In John 2:9-10, the master of the feast said to the servants that they should have put out the good wine at the beginning. In other words, the wine which the servants gave the guests at the start of the ceremony was bad wine (in the Scripture, the master of the feast used the word 'worse'). The master of the feast also said, 'You have kept the good wine until now.' This time he was talking about the wine that Jesus made. My question is: Is it not the same Jesus, who turned water into wine that says, 'He has come that we may have life more abundantly (John

10:10).' If Jesus truly has come that we might have life, He will not encourage us to take anything that is unclean and harmful. Jesus died that we might live (1 John 4:9). This shows that He loves and cares for us, and if He truly cares for us, He would not want us to drink alcohol (the killer), which He knows damages the brain, heart, liver, lungs, and kidneys. Lack of knowledge is like a disease, and many people are perishing because of it.

> *My people are destroyed for lack of knowledge. Because you have rejected knowledge, I also will reject you from being priest for Me; because you have forgotten the law of your God, I also will forget your children.*
>
> —*Hosea 4:6*
>
> *Most assuredly, I say to you, if anyone keeps My Word he shall never see death.*
>
> —*John 8:51*

Many marriages have been broken due to spouses' addiction to alcoholic drinks. To be addicted to alcohol does not depend on how long the person has been drinking it. In other words, a person can be addicted to alcohol from the moment they start to drink it. One percent of alcohol in a drink is still strong. When a person starts to drink alcohol gradually, it will become a habit. If the person continues drinking, his addiction will become worse. If the person does not seek help, his drinking habit will not only affect his life but his family and friends.

Story 3

Mr F and Ms M got married, and it lasted for twelve years. The marriage ended because Mr F was addicted to alcohol. Ms F gave him many opportunities to stop his alcoholic drinking, but he did not stop but continued to drink. When his drinking habit became worse, it affected both his family and friends. Mr F knew his family was suffering because of his drinking, yet he refused to quit. His wife had enough of him and could not leave with him anymore. She separated from him and later filed for divorce.

Story 4

Ms B was married to Mr H, and they lived together with their children for several years. Things started to change when Ms B began to drink. Ms B did not care or think about what her family was going through because of her alcohol addiction. As she continued to drink, her behaviour became worse and uncontrollable. One day, Ms B was unaware what she was doing and ran away from her matrimonial home to live with another man. As a result, the marriage came to an end.

> *Envy, murders, drunkenness, revelries, and the like; of which I tell you beforehand, just as I also told you in time past, that those who practice such things will not inherit the kingdom of God.*
>
> —*Galatians 5:21*

Story 5

Marriage is not a question of where the couple met before they got married, but whether they can live happily as husband and wife. Katie and Peter met in a TV reality show (*I'm a Celebrity, Get Me Out of Here*), began to date, and later got married. After their marriage the media asked whether the show was the right place to meet someone to marry. Unfortunately, the media did not get the right answer because they did not ask the right question. The media should have asked whether they were right for each other. If the answer is yes, there is no reason why they shouldn't be together. At the time of Peter and Katie's marriage, it appeared that Katie had a drinking problem, and it brought trouble between the pair. Before they got married, Peter must have known that Katie was an alcoholic. He should have sorted out Katie's drinking problems before taking their relationship further. However, after four and half years of marriage, Peter and Katie ended it in a very shameful way.

Do not get drunk on wine, which leads to debauchery [shamelessness]. Instead, be filled with the Spirit.
                                        —*Ephesians 5:18 (emphasis added)*

Story 6

If you are dating someone, and you know that their weakness will cause problems in the future, you should use their strength to fight the weakness. In our society today, many people reformed themselves because they wanted to be a better person in the future. President George W Bush was one of them; he said, "I owe my presidency to giving up drinking." He possessed a healthy marriage when he stopped drinking. Mr Bush spoke out his struggle with alcohol addiction, saying he would never have become US president had he not quit drinking. Mr Bush said he chose to go cold turkey more than twenty years ago when his drinking habit began to affect his family life. 'Alcohol can compete with your affections.' 'It sure it did in my case,' Mr Bush said in a US TV interview. 'It was the competition that I decided just wasn't worth it.' The former president added: 'I doubt I'd be standing here if I hadn't quit drinking whisky, beer, wine and all that.'

> *The thief does not come except to steal, and to kill, and to destroy. I have come that they may have life, and that they may have it more abundantly.*
>   —*John 10:10*

COUNSEL

A person does not have to be drunk before he accepts that he is an alcoholic. The thief does not come except to steal, kill, and destroy. Christians have to be very careful about what they eat or drink. They have to be aware of those things that the devil will use to harm their life. Jesus has come that you might have life more abundantly—that means you are fully guaranteed all of life. Your intention should be to live life to the fullest; you should not to allow the devil to destroy your life or matrimony. You must be filled with the Spirit so that you may know when God is speaking to you, for the enemy speaks with a convincing spirit: 'It does not matter; it is only a wine or a beer, and it contains less alcohol.'

Family members may be affected by alcohol differently. Parental alcoholism may affect the foetus even before a child is born. In pregnant women, alcohol is carried to all of the mother's organs and tissues, including the placenta, where it is easily crosses through the membrane separating the maternal and foetal blood system. When a pregnant woman drinks an alcoholic beverage, the concentration of alcohol in her unborn baby's bloodstream is the same level as her own. A pregnant woman who consumes alcohol during her pregnancy may give birth to a baby with Foetal Alcohol Syndrome.

If you have a spouse that drinks alcohol, and this is causing a problem in your marriage, do not panic and go to God in prayer. He already knows that you will face this kind of problem and that you will struggle while coping with it.

> *Come to Me, all you who labour and are heavy laden, and I will give you rest.*
> —Matthew 11:28

> *Take My yoke upon you and learn from Me, for I am gentle and lowly in heart, and you will find rest for your souls.*
> —Matthew 11:29

> *Call upon Me in the day of trouble; I will deliver you, and you shall glorify Me.*
> —Psalms 50:15

Story 7

Alcohol does not only affect families—it also kills those who consume it. There was an alcoholic man who died. When he died his lungs were donated and were transplanted to a patient. What the patient and her family did not know was that the deceased was an alcoholic. The truth emerged when the patient who received the lungs died a couple of weeks after her transplant. It was later revealed by the doctors that the patient died as a result of the affected alcoholic lungs.

The story above is a warning to all those who drink alcohol. You may not know the dangers of drinking alcohol, or the impact you will make to the generation after you. If you drink alcohol, your children will likely drink alcohol too; your children copy from you because you are their role model. They will think that because their parents drink alcohol, it is a good thing. If you do not tell them the risk of drinking alcohol or binge drinking, no one will. Do not let alcohol destroy you and your family.

Committing your spouse and their drinking problem to God is the only way you can make a difference in your spouse life and marriage. Do not shout at or fight with your spouse. Do not throw your spouse out of your matrimonial home. Do not tell everyone about your spouse's drinking problem. Do not make your spouse feel rejected. Do not make your spouse think you are making things worse by behaving irrational towards them (which will only increase the drinking habit).

> The wise woman builds her house, but the foolish pulls it down with her hands.
>
> *—Proverbs 14:1*

You and your spouse are one. You must help your spouse beat the drinking habit. First you must find out how your spouse started to drink and why. Your spouse's drinking habit may have started as a result of heritage (i.e., inherited from one or both parents) or because of the company he/she keeps. Your spouse's drinking may have started because your spouse goes to clubs or pubs. It could also be a result of no job or stress at work. Whatever the reason is, there is nothing too hard for God to do.

> Ah, Lord God! Behold, You have made the heavens and the earth by Your great power and outstretched arm. There is nothing too hard for You.
>
> *—Jeremiah 32:17*

It is important to know the origin of a problem before tackling it because the knowledge will help you to focus your prayers on the crucial side rather than the ordinary. When you find out how or where your spouse started his drinking problem, pray to remove the root of that problem. When you have done this, the yoke will be broken, and the burden will be taken away from your shoulders.

> It shall come to pass in that day that his burden will be taken away from your shoulder and his yoke from your neck, and the yoke will be destroyed because of the anointing.
> —Isaiah 10:27

If you have a friend (a believer) that supports you spiritually or you think you can trust, fast and pray earnestly with that person concerning your spouse's drinking, because there things that cannot be solved except through praying and fasting ('So He said to them, "This kind can come out by nothing but prayer and fasting." Mark 9:29). It is also good that you pray in an agreement, for quick prayer answers ('Again I say to you that if two of you agree on earth concerning anything that they ask, it will be done for them by My Father in heaven.' Matthew 18:19).

Six

Love of Money

VI

Love of Money

*M*oney *is an implement* on which people depend to control every facet of their lives. Money is so vital that many think that if they do not have it, they cannot live or enjoy life to their expectations. There is no doubt about the influence of money because if people do not have it, they cannot live a life that is enriched with meaning and filled with optimism. Money is a necessity, but it can be a detriment if people do not obtain it in the right manner. Money itself is not evil—it's when people start to think of evil ways to get it that it becomes evil in the eyes of the Almighty God. The importance of having money and means of getting is crucial. People should work to obtain money rather than getting it some other way.

> *For even when we were with you, we commanded you this: If anyone will not work, neither shall he eat.*
> —*2 Thessalonians 3:10*

The real worth of money makes it possible for us to have those things that make life more enjoyable—things like being able to have your own home, better education, and good health, as well as providing for our families and self, feeding the poor, sponsoring the preaching of the gospel of Christ, maintaining the house of God, and more. All these are good reasons for having money.

Although money can provide people food, shelter, education, and safety, it cannot buy love and happiness. Many people love money so much that they have made it equivalent to their happiness. They are more susceptible to many lustful temptations because of their love for money. The love of money has compelled many people to selfish and greedy behaviours, and their desire to be rich leads them into evil; they lie, cheat, bribe, deceive, induce, defame, slander, and even kill to get it. The love of money becomes the ultimate idolatry. This is why Apostle Paul said the love of money is the root of all evil.

> *For the love of money is a root of all kinds of evil, for which some have strayed from the faith in their greediness, and pierced themselves through with many sorrows.*
> —*1 Timothy 6:10*

The passage implies that all immorality and wickedness is caused by people loving money, not by money itself. The root is greed, the desire to be rich. Riches are neither good nor bad; it is the attitude towards them that is good or bad. Apostle Paul said to Timothy, 'Charge them that are rich to trust only in the living God and not uncertain riches.'

> *Command those who are rich in this present age not to be haughty, nor to trust in uncertain riches but in the living God, who gives us richly all things to enjoy.*
> —*1 Timothy 6:17*

> *Whoever trusts in his riches will fall, but the righteous will thrive like a green leaf.*
> —*Proverbs 11:28*

Love of money has to do with a person putting their trust in it. What a person puts their trust in is what they serve. No one can serve two masters at the same time. You either hate one or love the other or you be loyal to one and despise the other. In other words, you cannot love God and money. God is not a God that is prepared to share you with the world. Therefore, Christians should not bow down nor serve things of this world, because the Almighty is a jealous God.

> *No one can serve two masters; for either he will hate the one and love the other, or else he will be loyal to the one and despise the other. You cannot serve God and mammon.*
> —*Matthew 6:24*

You shall not bow down to them nor serve them. For I, the Lord your God, am a jealous God, visiting the iniquity of the fathers upon the children to the third and fourth generations of those who hate Me.

　　　　　　　　　　　　　　　　　—Exodus 20:5

Story 1

Ms J met a man, who was very wealthy. They started dating each other, and later broke up, and got back together shortly after their broke up. But this time they decided to take their relationship further to marital. One year after they got married, they got divorced. Ms J was never in love with the man but was only interested in his riches. Her reason for marrying and divorcing the rich man was because she wants his money.

The love of money is caused by the lust of the eyes.

The lust of the eyes obviously refers to what is seen, or what you want to see. The eyes enjoy things of riches or wealth, and when people lust after those worldly things, it is the lust of the eyes. Christians should change their heart for God, and constantly do their best to live for Him. If Christians change their heart for the world, their desires are for the things, which the world offers, and that is the time they are guilty of the "lust of the eyes."

Do not love the world or the things in the world. If anyone loves the world, the love of the Father is not in him.

　　　　　　　　　　　　　　　　　—1 John 2:15

For all that is in the world, the lust of the flesh, the lust of the eyes, and the pride of life is not of the Father, but is of the world.

　　　　　　　　　　　　　　　　　—1 John 2:16

Story 2

Mr S was sent by his employers to another country to live and work. He was paid thousands of pounds every month. One day, Mr S met Ms E, a prostitute, and then started to date her. During their courtship, Mr S was paying Ms E one thousand pounds every month. Later they got married and had two children.

Mr S was unaware that his wife was having an affair with two other men from her country. However, when he suspected that something was not right, he then told Ms E that he was going on a business trip. Mr S left the house, hid at a corner, and filmed Ms E. Ms E thought that Mr S has left the building and invited his friends to come over. They partied all day and were intoxicated.

When Mr S returned home, he did not waste time but spontaneously asked for divorce, and he stopped Ms E's monthly allowance. Mr S moved out of his matrimonial home to live with one of his colleagues. One night, while Mr S was still living with his friend, two men came inside his friend's house and shot him dead. When the police got involved, they found out that Ms E married Mr S because of his money. This was the time it emerged that Ms E was having an affair with the two men (Mr S's murderers) before he met Mr S. Ms E and the men thought that they only way they could get Mr S's money were for Ms E to marry Mr S. Ms E and those two murderers are currently serving life sentences.

In the twilight, in the evening, in the black and dark night:
—*Proverbs 7:9*

For she sits at the door of her house, on a seat by the highest places of the city.
—*Proverbs 9:14*

To call to those who pass by, who go straight on their way.
—*Proverbs 9:15*

Passing along the street near her corner; and he took the path to her house.

—Proverbs 7:8

And there a woman met him, with the attire of a harlot [prostitute], and a crafty heart.

—Proverbs 7:10 (emphasis added))

So she caught him, and kissed him, with an impudent face she said to him.

—Proverbs 7:13

I have perfumed my bed with myrrh, aloes, and cinnamon.

—Proverbs 7:17

Come, let us take our fill of love until the morning; let us delight ourselves with love.

—Proverbs 7:18

With her enticing speech she caused him to yield, with her flattering lips she seduced him.

—Proverbs 7:21

Immediately he went after her, as an ox goes to the slaughter or as a fool to the correction of the stocks.

—Proverbs 7:22

Till an arrow struck his liver, as a bird hastens to the snare, he did not know it would cost his life.

—Proverbs 7:23

But he does not know that the dead are there, that her guests are in the depths of hell.

—Proverbs 9:18

Now therefore, listen to me, my children; pay attention to the Words of My mouth.

—Proverbs: 7:24

Do not let your heart turn aside to her ways; do not stray into her paths.

—*Proverbs 7:25*

For she has cast down many wounded, and all who were slain by her were strong men.

—*Proverbs 7:26*

Her house is the way to hell, descending to the chambers of death.

—*Proverbs 7:27*

What was Mr S thinking when he got married to a prostitute? He had a good job and everything going for him. When Mr S started to date the harlot, he became a different person. According to his friends and family, Mr S genuine believed that Ms E was the right one, the woman he could trust to be his wife and mother of his children. He convinced himself that he would change her to be a better woman. His colleagues at work warned him about his relationship with her, but he paid no heed to it. He lavished money on Ms E and her parents *(Whosoever loves wisdom makes his father rejoice, but a companion of harlots wastes his wealth, Proverbs 29:3).* Despite everything Mr S did for Ms E and her family, still she planned for his murder.

There is a way which seems right unto a man, but the end there of are the ways of death.

—*Proverbs 14: 12*

My son, give attention to my words; incline your ear to my sayings.

—*Proverbs 4:20*

Do not let them depart from your eyes; keep them in the midst of your heart;

—*Proverbs 4:21*

The story of Mr S was a tragic one and a warning to all those men sleeping with or dating prostitutes. Prostitutes do not stay with one man; what takes prostitutes outside will always bring them inside. Ms E's evil behaviour shows that people can do anything for the love of money. Her plan was to kill Mr S and acquire his money and assets. A pure reputation should be one's goal in life rather than acquiring riches (*A good name is more desirable than great riches; to be esteemed is better than silver and gold, Proverbs 22:1*). Ms E succeeded in murdering Mr S but lost the money and her children. Her greediness and unfaithfulness took her to jail, where she would spend the rest of her life.

> *Who can find a virtuous woman? For her worth is far above rubies.*
> —*Proverbs 31:10*

> *The heart of her husband safely trusts her; so he will have no lack of gain.*
> —*Proverbs 31:11*

> *She does him good and not evil, all the days of her life.*
> —*Proverbs 31:12*

Story 3

Mr D was a successful businessman and was happily married with children. His marriage started to experience problems when he began to have an affair with one of his customers, Ms P. Mr D was always taking her out for lunch and dinner, and he also showered her with gifts. Ms P knew that Mr D had a wife and children, but because of her love for money, she didn't care to end the relationship. Later Mr D divorced her wife and married Ms P, who bore two children for him.

Mr D's eldest children left home because they did not get along with their step-mother. The younger children remained with their father but also did not get on with their step-mum. They fought with her all the time, and as a result they brawled with their father. The children, their father, and their step-mother's relationships had become worse. I advised Ms P to end their marriage because she was committing adultery, but she refused to act upon my advice.

Each time I visited Ms P, I preached the Gospel and cited from the Scripture on what God said about marriage and divorce. God ministered to some brethren regarding Mr D's relationship with Ms P. God urged Mr D to take back his wife and warned him that if anything happened to her wife, her blood would be on his hand. Mr D ignored God's warning and continued to live with his second wife.

Some years later, Mr D came back to his senses—but this was after he had sold everything he owed with his first wife and had nothing left to sell. His eyes were opened, and he knew the truth about God's Word concerning marriage *(And you shall know the truth and the truth shall make you free, John 8:32)*. He begged his first wife to return and did not waste time to ask his second wife to leave.

When Mr D's wife returned to their matrimonial home, Mr D apologised to her. Unfortunately, it was too late because his wife did not recover from an illness that was a result of their divorce. After the death of Mr D's first wife, his children scattered, and their father was nowhere to be found. The second wife, whose son died during her relationship with Mr D, left with her daughter to live with another man in another city.

> *You have heard it was said to those of old, you shall not commit adultery.*
> —*Matthew 5:27*

> *So He said to them, whoever divorces his wife and marries commits adultery*
> —*Mark 10:11*

> *And if a woman divorces her husband and marries another, she commits adultery against her*
> —*Mark 10:12*

Whoever marries a divorcee commits adultery.
—Matthew 5:32b

'For the LORD God of Israel says that He hates divorce, for it covers one's garment with violence,' Says the LORD of hosts. 'Therefore take heed to your spirit that you do not deal treacherously.'
—Malachi 2: 16

But whoever commits adultery with a woman lacked understanding; he who does so destroys his own soul.
—Proverbs 6:32

Now the works of the flesh are evident, which are adultery, fornication, uncleanness, lasciviousness.
—Galatians 5:19

I have also told you in time past that those who do practice such things will not inherit the kingdom of God.
—Galatians 5:21b

One of the examples of disapproved relationship in the Scripture was that of Abraham and Hagar. God knew very well that such a relationship was not right, and it did not matter that Hagar had a son for Abraham. When Sarah was not happy with Hagar and wanted her out of their matrimonial home, God told Abraham to listen to his wife. Sarah was the one and only approved wife for Abraham.

But God said to Abraham, 'Do not let it be displeasing in your sight because of the lad or because of your bondwoman. Whatever Sarah has said to you, listens to her voice; for in Isaac your seed shall be called.'
—Genesis 21:12

Whatever people do that may be right in their eyes, it may not be right in the eyes of God. God is not a God of separation but a God of unification. God is not a God of division but a God of unity. Marriage is a commitment—for better or for worse, until death do you part. It does not matter if your wife has a problem conceiving; she is your wife, and God recognises her as your one and only wife. If your wife gives birth to children, whether they are male or female, God recognises them as the heir of the family. A husband with one wife is what God sees as a good marriage. The Word of God permits you to remarry only when your spouse is dead, but only in the Lord.

> *A bishop then must be blameless, the husband of one wife, temperate, sober-minded, of good behaviour, hospitable, able to teach.*
>
> *—1 Timothy 3:2*

> *One who rules his own house well, having his children in submission with all reverence.*
>
> *—1 Timothy 3:4*

> *For if a man does not know how to rule his own house, how will he take care of the church of God?*
>
> *—1 Timothy 3:5*

> *Let deacons be the husband of one wife, ruling their children and their own houses well.*
>
> *—1 Timothy 3:12*

> *A wife is bound by law as long as her husband lives; but if her husband dies, she is at liberty to be married to whom she wishes, only in the Lord.*
>
> *—1 Corinthians 7:39*

COUNSEL

Marriage is no longer perceived in the manner God wants it to be seen. The majority of people marry for the love of money rather than in the name of love. Those who marry for the love of money see marriage as a business: what they would gain or profit if they get married. No matter how much money they think they would gain or profit in a marriage, it is sure that such riches will certainly not bring joy and happiness. What brings joy and happiness in a relationship is the love the couple has for each other. Love should be the overriding reason to be with someone.

If you marry someone because of their riches, and the marriage breaks up and the rich person takes the money and leaves you with nothing, what are you going to do? You would certainly look for another rich person, and if you don't get one, you would be miserable the rest of your life. Furthermore, if you marry for the love of money, you will be making a big error because you will never be happy, and it will be to your detriment.

The fact that some wives love money more than their husbands is at times the fault of the rich men. Why? There is a website for women who are interested in dating rich men. This is a relationship that would lead to marriage, and it is only for men who are willing to spend and for women, who love money. If you want a successful and lasting marriage, you will not be interested in such ungodly relationship. The men and women who are members of the website are only interested in what they would gain, and not what they would bring in the relationship to make it healthy and perfect. It is obvious that women who want money and not love would join the website. Such websites proves that rich people, especially men, prefer to marry women who love money.

> There is a way that seems right to a man, but in the end it leads to death.
> —Proverbs 14:12

Spouses who have maintained a long relationship are not together because of their wealth but for the love they have for each other. Though money is something, it is not everything. In other words, money can buy you a lot of things, but it cannot buy you love, joy, happiness, righteousness, or a virtuous woman. Men who think they can marry any woman they want because they have money are deluding themselves, and they also will not have a long-lasting marriage. Men who want to have a successful marriage must be submissive to the Lordship of the Word of God. They've got to know the Word and let the Word guide their thoughts, their words, and all they do, for a virtuous woman is worth than money and riches.

> Who can find a virtuous wife? For her worth is far above rubies.
> —Proverbs 31:10

House and riches are an inheritance from fathers and a prudent
wife is from the Lord.

—*Proverbs 19:14*

A spouse who loves you is willing to spend the rest of his or her life with you
(with or without money), whereas a spouse who does not love you is more
interested in living with you as long as you are willing to spend your cash
on him/her. Those who marry for the love of money always have their eyes
on someone else. When the money finishes, they will leave their spouse for
someone that can provide that cash they need. But if they decide to continue
in the relationship, they will be committing all sorts of atrocity to fulfil their
egoism. They can never settle with one person because their main target in
relationship is to get money, rather than to receive love. Do not marry a man
or woman because he/she is rich. Marry because of love.

Seven

Lack of Love and Care

VII

Lack of Love and Care

In the beginning God created the heaven and the earth. After the earth He created every other thing before creating man. Why was man last? So that man would lack nothing. Everything man needed to satisfy himself on earth was created before him. The Scripture told us that man was created in the image of God. God, by creating man in His similarity, shows that the Almighty God loves man so much. God could have made man in any picture; He could have chosen not to create man at all. God could have created the animals alone to rule the earth, but He did not. After the creation of man, God gave man dominion over all the creatures. He bestowed man with the ability to rule, control, reign, dictate, govern, and manage all the creatures. This is true love.

> *Then God said, 'Let Us make man in our image, according to our likeness; let them have dominion over the fish of the sea, over the birds of the air, and over the cattle, over all the earth and over every creeping thing that creeps on the earth.'*
> —Genesis 1:26

There are several ways to define love. Love it is defined as a strong feeling that you have when you like somebody very much. It is the emotion of strong affection and personal attachment. In philosophical context, love is a virtue representing all human kindness, compassion, and affection. In spiritual context, love is not just a virtue but the basis for all being, as in the biblical phrase, 'God is love.' Love may also be defined as actions towards others (or oneself) based on compassion or affection.

The Christian understanding is that love comes from God. The love of man and woman (Eros in Greek) and the unselfish love of others (agape) are often contrasted as 'ascending' and 'descending' love, respectively, but they are ultimately the same thing. The Scripture says, 'Love is patient, love is kind. It does not envy, it does not boast, it is not proud. It not rude, it is not self-seeking, it is not easily angered, it keeps no record of wrongs. Love does not delight in evil but rejoices with the truth. It always protects, always trusts, always hopes, and always perseveres' (1 Corinthians. 13:4-7).

The secular world loves differently. They love conditionally and because of what they get from you, and anytime you cease to give to them, they discontinue loving you. This is not love but the bondage of love (or yoke of love). Bondage of love is when a person has to offer something to people in order to be loved or accepted by them.

> *We know that we have passed from death to life, because we love the brethren. He who does not love his brother abides in death.*
> *—1 John 3:14*

> *Whoever hates his brother is a murderer, and you know that no murderer has eternal life abiding in him.*
> *—1 John 3:15*

> *If someone says, 'I love God,' and hates his brother, he is a liar; for he who does not love his brother whom he has seen, how can he love God whom he has not seen?*
> *—1 John 4:20*

> *No one has seen God at any time. If we love one another, God abides in us, and His love has been perfected in us.*
> *—1 John 4:12*

The majority of men spend a lot of money on women, merely for the women to love them. Some women sleep with the men because they think that then the men will love them. This is not the kind of love that God expected from His children to give to others. Christians are expected to love all people, even if they do not love them back.

Christians ought to love unconditionally and unselfishly, without limits and conditions. Christians should not love people because others love them first, or because of what they get from them. Christians must love because the Word of God commands us to love our neighbours as ourselves.

> *For if you love those who love you, what rewards have you? Do not even the tax collectors do the same?*
> —*Matthew 5:46*

> *Dear friends, let us love one another, for love comes from God. Everyone who loves has been born of God and knows God.*
> —*1 John 4:7*

> *He that loves not knows not God; for God is love.*
> —*1 John 4:8*

> *Dear friends, since God so loved us, we also ought to love one another.*
> —*1 John 4:11*

> *No-one has ever seen God; but if we love one another, God lives in us and his love is made complete in us.*
> —*1 John 4:12*

> *And the second, like it, is this: 'You shall love your neighbour as yourself.' There is no other commandment greater than these.*
> —*Mark 12:31*

A true love comes from the heart, it is freely given, and you do not pay anything to receive it. This was the kind of love God had to double for us. After God created man in His likeness, His love for man did not stop. However, He had to double His extraordinary love for man by giving the world His one and only precious Son, so that man can be saved, and also through His Son, man might live. Sending Jesus into the world was not due to our request or because of our goodness or holiness. It was because of the pure and unconditional love God had for each and every one of us. Notwithstanding that we have sinned and fall short of the glory of God, He sent His beloved Son to be the propitiation of our sins. God is a loving Father, and His love is flawless. The unconditional love He has for us has never weakened but has always been unwavering.

> *For God so loved the world that He gave His only begotten Son, that whoever believes in Him should not perish but have everlasting life.*
> —*John 3:16*

> *This is how God showed his love among us: He sent his one and only Son into the world that we might live through him.*
> —*1 John 4:9*

> *But God demonstrates His own love toward us, in that while we were still sinners, Christ died for us.*
> —*Romans 5:8*

> *For all have sinned and fall short of the glory of God.*
> —*Romans 3:23.*

> *This is love: not that we loved God, but that he loved us and sent his Son as an atoning sacrifice for our sins.*
> —*1 John 4:10*

There is no doubt that marriages fail due to lack of love and care between spouses. The lack of love and care between spouses is sometimes caused by one or both spouses having missed out on parental love while growing up. People who were never loved by their parents find it difficult to love others. It is imperative that couples love their children so that when they grow up and get married, they will have no problem loving their spouses and children. When a child misses parental love, it does have an effect on that child, especially when the child becomes an adult. Some of them, when they get married, find it difficult to love their spouse but when it comes to loving their children, they have no problem.

Story 1

A famous musician claimed that he was never loved by his father and was always beaten and hit by his father. He showed agony when he complained about missing his childhood and that he never felt what it was like to be a child. His first and second marriages did not work but ended very badly. He did not marry again; however, he had children with different women. When he was alive he loved his children so much but did not want anything to do with their biological mothers.

A lawyer asked Jesus, 'Teacher which is the great commandment in law.' Jesus said to him, 'You shall love the Lord your God with all your heart, with all your soul and with your entire mind.' This is the first and great commandment, and the second is like it: 'You shall love your neighbour as yourself' *(Matthew22:35-39)*. The question is: how can a husband and wife who do not love each other love another person who is not close to them. The simple answer is they must first love their dearest (charity begins at home) before they can love those who are not related to them. The Scripture says that those who do not show love towards others have no knowledge of God *(1 John 4:8)*.

If Jesus commanded you to love your neighbour, how much love would you think He would want you to give to your spouse that He has connected to you? Without doubt He would want you to love your spouse in the same manner you love and cherish yourself. The Word of God says love your neighbour and fellow citizens as yourself. However, your spouse is not just your fellow citizen but your own flesh; therefore you have to love your spouse more than you have ever loved anyone, and it should be exactly the same way you adore yourself. Furthermore, spouses should bear in mind that their other half is no dissimilarity from their body. In other words, their spouse is the same as them. They also must love their spouse in the manner Christ loves the Church.

> *So husbands ought to love their own wives as their own bodies; he who loves his wife loves himself.*
>
> *—Ephesians 5:28*

For no one ever hated his own flesh, but nourishes and cherishes it, just as the Lord does the Church.

—*Ephesians 5:29*

Husbands love your wives, just as Christ also loved the Church and gave Himself for her.

—*Ephesians 5:25*

A husband and wife who are in love with each other do not dishonour their bed. However, if one spouse is found to be unfaithful, the other spouse will forgive because of the love and care they have for each other. It is true that spouses who cheat on their spouse are adulterers, which is a sin. But if you are a child of God, you will forgive those who trespass against you, and an adulterer is no exception. In the Scripture, Jesus forgave a prostitute named Mary Magdalene (John 8:3-11). Spouses must forgive their spouse who committed adultery against them, and they also should continue to love and care for them.

But if you do not forgive, neither will your Father in heaven forgive your trespasses.

—*Mark 11:26*

So My heavenly Father also will do to you if each of you, from his heart, does not forgive his brother his trespasses.

—*Matthew 18:35*

And forgive us our debts, as we forgive our debtors.

—*Matthew 6:12*

The rule for forgiveness is that everyone must forgive up to seventy times seven. In other words, husbands and wives must forgive their spouses for each sin they committed against them. It does not matter that a particular sin hurts more than other sins; couples must forgive their spouses. All sins are equal—no sin is smaller or bigger! That means that all sinful, immoral or amoral acts, including adultery, are the same and must be forgiven in the same manner. In addition, it is important that couples confess their faults and pray for their spouses so they can settle their differences and have a winning marriage.

Then Peter came to Him and said, 'Lord, how often shall my brother sin against me, and I forgive him? Up to seven times?'
—*Matthew 18:21*

Jesus said to him, 'I do not say to you, up to seven times, but up to seventy times seven.'
—*Matthew 18:22*

For whoever shall keep the whole law, and yet stumble in one point, he is guilty of all.
—*James 2:10*

Whoever commits sin also commits lawlessness, and sin is lawlessness.
—*1 John 3:4*

Confess your trespasses to one another, and pray for one another, that you may be healed. The effective, fervent prayer of a righteous man avails much.
—*James 5:16*

Story 2

Mr H and Ms W had been married for fifteen years and had two children. Ms W was never at home because she was always busy at work; she was more committed to her job than her marriage. Whenever Ms W returned home from work, she was always tired and did not sit down and chat with her husband. Her husband was not happy with her and refused to sleep with her. He spent most of his time alone, thinking about their marriage breakdown. Afterwards he resigned from work to become a househusband, in order to look after their children. Opportunities for higher positions in his career were offered to him, and he turned them down. One day, a letter came from the post addressed to Ms W; she opened it and saw it was a divorce letter. In the letter her husband had asked her to leave their matrimonial home. Ms W was shocked! She could not believe what she had just read. She called Mr H immediately and tried to explain why she had not been there for him and their kids, but Mr H could not look at her or patiently listen to her. Mr H felt it was too late to forgive his wife because he tried to make it work, but their marriage problem was getting worse. He later divorced Ms W.

Spouses generally experience problems in marriage. Nevertheless, love conquers all. Spouses should not look at the problems they face in their marriage; they should look at their spouse and remember the first day they met, and the day they stood before God and said 'I do.' They should remember what they said to each other, their agreed vows—that is, for better or for worse, till death do they part. This promise came from the heart and showed a genuine love from the heart, a true friendship and relationship. It showed that both of them were willing to become husband and wife, willing to face challenges and overlook faults no matter what.

It is true that some conduct hurts, especially when the wrongdoer is someone you love and trust. However, what you are going through is nothing to compare to what Jesus went through for this world. He was wounded for your transgression. He was bruised for your iniquities. He was abused and chastised! It was painful! It was agonizing! It was aching! It was stinging! It was bitter! It was sore! It was harrowing! It was cruel! It was traumatic! It was vexing! It was sorrowful! It was unpleasant! It was ruthless! Yet He stood. Do you know there was a moment that Jesus wanted to give up, but when He remembered you, He remembered what would happen to you if He did not steadfast and overcome? This was the reason why He took all the abuse, marriage problems, and all the problems that you are facing now, and nailed them on the cross and became victorious, the moment He said, 'It is finished.'

Jesus went from sovereignty to shame and from deity to death. Why? For you! Everything Jesus went through was because of the love He had for you, and He still loves you. If you think it is difficult to love and care for your spouse or family, especially when they have offended you; you should think about what Jesus had to suffer because of you. Most couples experience problems in their marriage because they do not love and care for their spouse in the same manner Jesus loves and cares for them. Husbands and wives should be devoted to one another.

> _Be devoted to one another brotherly love. Honour one another above yourselves._
> —Romans 12:10

> _Love must be sincere. Hate what is evil; cling to what is good._
> —Romans 12:9

Forgiveness is the only answer to transgression. If spouses want to defeat the enemy troubling their marital life, they must continue to forgive and love their spouse each time they offend them. The devil is an enemy to love and forgiveness. The devil hates those who forgive their spouse. He hates to see happy, married couples enjoying a peaceful marital life. The devil hates the fact that spouses want to have a healthy and successful marriage, and he is doing everything in his power to cause problems between spouses. Married couples must not give the devil the chance to come between them. The devil will always cause trouble, but once spouses refuse to submit to his demands, he will carry his load and flee from their marriage (_'therefore submit to God. Resist the devil and he will flee from you,'_ James 4:7). Furthermore, spouses must not carry the burden of sin, so that they can overcome their trials and tribulation. If spouses have a chip on their shoulder, the Heavenly Father will not forgive them of their transgression.

> _And whenever you stand praying, if you have anything against anyone, forgive him that your Father in heaven may also forgive you your trespasses._
> —Mark 11:25

> _Bear with each other and forgive whatever grievances you may have against one another. Forgive as the Lord forgave you._
> —Colossians 3:13

Most men put their jobs first before their wives. They have prayed and asked God to secure a job for them, and He did. Now they are telling God that the job is a problem. It is a problem indeed, because the job must not come first, before the wife. A beloved wife is primary and the job is secondary. If your job has taken over your time and life, leave it, because it is not worthy. It may be your source of income, but it is not the reason you are living. Christ is the reason you are living, and if He has blessed you with a wife, you must love and care for her. There are many men looking for a wife like yours, and they are unable to find one. Men, adore your wife and not your job. Love your wife and not your job. Spend more time with your wife than you do with your job, and do not let your job become important than your wife. Remember, he who found a wife has found a good thing.

> *He who finds a wife finds a good thing, and obtains favour*
> *from the Lord.*
> —*Proverbs 18:22*

Some couples behave differently towards their spouse once a baby arrives. When the first or second child arrives, the love the spouses have for each other begins to weaken. As for the women, they will no longer care for or pay attention to their husbands; this is because the love and care they have for their husband has been transferred to the newborn. Thus, they will concentrate on the newborn and will not bother to show any affection towards their husband. Some women will not want to stay near their husband but will get angry when he is around. They will behave poorly towards their husband and will not care if he eats. They will starve him, using the newborn child as an excuse for not be able to provide or prepare food for him. As a result, the man will start to eat outside. When the man starts eating outside, one day he will end up eating from another woman's pot.

Men are not dissimilar to women when a newborn arrives. Most men discontinue loving and caring for their wives because they have lose interest in their wives. They will stop the support and help they give to her, and they will not care if she is in need of anything. The man's main focus will be only on the newborn child. The man will pamper the child as if it is the only one he has in the world. Men will forget that without their wives, the baby would not have come in the first place. Children are the reward of the womb and also gifts from God. No child has the right to take the place of its parents.

Story 3

When Mr V and Ms O met, Ms O was convinced that Mr V was madly in love with her. Mr V used to treat Ms O like a diamond. Whatever she requested or wanted was provided by her man. But when they started to have kids, Mr V's attitude towards her was something she never imagined. He changed from the man she knew to a man she never knew. Mr V liked to spend most of his time on the computer, and when he was not on the computer he was with their kids or at work. He cared about his children but not in the same way he cared about Ms O. They didn't sit down and talk like couples should. Mr V did not help her, except to pay the rent and bills. Food and other necessities were provided by Ms C. Ms C did the domestic work and prepared food in the house. When she was pregnant and needed support from Mr V, she did not receive the help she requested from him. Mr V complained that he paid the rent and bills, so the rest was up to Ms C. Due to lack of love, care, support, and communication, Ms C was not happy in their relationship, and she considered leaving Mr V.

God can never give you a spouse that will not love and care for you. God is a loving Dad and an expert when it comes to choosing the right spouse. He created you and knows the best spouse for you. When you neglect Him and choose your spouse by yourself, you will have problems later in your marriage. However, if you find someone you like and commit that person or your relationship to God, He will make you see sense. He will reveal to you whether that person is the right one for you. Once again, God is a loving and caring Father who knows what is best for His children. He will always give you someone who will cherish and look after you. What God gives you makes you rich and causes no grief.

> *The blessing of the Lord makes one rich, and He add no sorrow with it.*
>
> *—Proverbs 10:22*

COUNSEL

Praying together as a couple and praying individually for your spouse is one of the most powerful weapons you have against divorce and in favour of building intimacy in your marriage. If you really want to have a successful marriage, you must always love, care, support, and pray for your spouse. There is no doubt that couples do have problems in marriage, but love conquers all. In a relationship where you are bound with love and care, things work simply and smoothly, and you can easily solve problems that might arise in your marriage. But if both of you have no love and care for each other, you will have difficulties tackling the problems alone by yourself.

> Two are better than one; because they have a good reward for their labour.
>
> —Ecclesiastes 4:9

> For if they fall one, will lift up his companion but woe to him who is alone when he falls, for he has no one to help him up.
>
> —Ecclesiastes 4:10

People who had no parental love find it difficult to love and care for their spouse, because they were never loved and cared for by their own parents. When you don't give or receive love from your spouse, it will not only affect your relationship but also the relationship between you and your children. Your past experiences might have been worse than your nightmares; however, you should not dwell in the past. You must forget your past experience and move on, for the sake of your family and God. Furthermore, if your paternal or maternal relatives never loved or cared for you, let it go and do not allow it to affect your marital life. Be a good example to those who might have experienced the same childhood neglect, by loving and caring for your spouse and children. Those who stay in love stay in God, and God is in them.

> And we have known and believed the love that God has for us. God is love, and he who abides in love abides in God and God in him.
>
> —1 John 4:16

Many spouses feel second class in their marriage because of the way they are being treated by their other half. You should not feel inferior to your spouse, and neither should your spouse make you feel less important in your marriage. Your spouse should always remain that special person in your life. He/she should not be treated like an ordinary person on the street, but preciously like royalty. You must treat your spouse with respect, even when you are in the company of others. If you do not respect your spouse, then others (including your children, parents, siblings, and friends) will not treat your spouse with respect. Do not speak to your spouse in the manner you speak to your children. Do not raise your voice when talking to your spouse, as your children might copy you. You must always speak to your spouse with love and not with pride. Getting rid of arrogance and pride makes a marriage successful.

When you shown love to others, whatever you ask God in your prayers, He will do it (And whatever we ask we receive from Him, because we keep His commandments and do those things that are pleasing in His sight. And this is His commandment: that we should believe on the name of His Son Jesus Christ and love one another, as He gave us commandment (1 John 3:22-23). You must love everyone, but the love you have for your spouse must be different and special because your spouse takes precedence over everyone else. If you have no love for your spouse, it shows you do not love yourself because you and your spouse share one body (So husbands ought to love their own wives as their own bodies; he who loves his wife loves himself. For no one ever hated his own flesh, but nourishes and cherishes it, just as the Lord does the church—Ephesians 5:28-29). Furthermore, you should always spend quality time with your spouse. If your spouse does not get your full attention, he/she will go somewhere else to get it. Do not let your spouse seek attention from an outsider, if you want your marriage to be a victorious one.

Most spouses put their career, job, or business before their spouse. If you are one of them, stop it, because you are not doing the right thing. Your career is secondary, and your spouse must be your first priority. To have a career is very good, but when it affects the relationship between you and your spouse, it is not good.

Every spouse needs the love and support of their spouse to make their career or business become successful. You need your spouse as much as your spouse needs you to flourish in everything you do. It does not matter that you already had a successful career before you met your spouse; to be vastly successful, you need more than a career. In other words, you need your spouse's support (or comfort) to be on top. In addition, it is not good to have too many career ambitions because those who are career ambitious do not always have a long-lasting relationship.

Story 4

Mrs C was a married woman who started well in her career. However, when she became career ambitious, she started losing her role as a wife. She was so determined to be famous and was willing to do anything to achieve it and be on top. Due to her career ambitions, her husband was not getting enough love from her and therefore started to sleep with strange women (including prostitutes). When she found out, she was furious and heartbroken. She separated from her husband and then filed for divorce.

> The wise woman builds her house, but the foolish pulls it down with her hands.
>
> —Proverbs 14:1

These days, there are many selfish spouses who do not care for their spouse's needs. Selfishness is a sin. A child of God should not be egoistic but must look after others and care for their needs. When you care for others, including your spouse, God will take care of you and your situation. When you put your needs before your spouse's needs, you are not creating a loving and caring atmosphere in your marriage. Spouses must be considerate towards each other, especially when it comes to their needs in marriage. Your needs and that of your spouse have to be measured equally, and the love and care you have for each other must be the same. Additionally, spouses must not refuse each other love making, as this is a necessity in marriage. If you refuse to make love to your other half, your spouse will go hunting.

Story 5

I met a woman who was so distraught in her marriage. She told me that her husband commits adultery. She was so annoyed that she was considering divorcing him. Later in the story, I comprehended that her husband wants to make love to her and also wants another child, but she refused to consider her husband's needs (she was more interested in obtaining her husband's country citizenship than saving her matrimony). When her husband couldn't get what was due to him, he went outside to sleep with other women to satisfy his needs.

> Let the husband render to his wife the affection due her, and likewise also the wife to her husband.
> —*1 Corinthians 7:3*

> The wife does not have authority over her own body, but the husband does. And likewise the husband does not have authority over his own body, but the wife does.
> —*1 Corinthians 7:4*

> Do not deprive one another except with consent for a time that you may give yourselves to fasting and praying; and come together again so that Satan does not tempt you because of your lack of self-control.
> —*1 Corinthians 7:5*

Eight

Religions

VIII

Religions

While things like religion are frequently swept under the rug during the period of courtship and early marriage, they can often creep up and cause problems later on. Religion is often described for the coherence of belief, focusing on a system of unseen beings, persons, or objects that are considered to be supernatural, sacred, divine, or of the highest truth. Religion is also described as the belief in a god or gods and the activities connected with this (this includes idols crafted by men, carved image of any likeness of anything made in heaven or on earth). Therefore anything created by men or God that is seen by people as something to give reverence to, is a god. Those who worship or bow to these gods—whether it is images of anything in heaven, on earth, and in water—are not obeying the Word of God. The Word of God says that we should not have any other gods before Him because the Almighty God is a jealous God.

> *You shall have no other gods before me.*
>
> *—Exodus 20:3*

> *You shall not make for yourself a carved image any likeness of anything that is in heaven above, or that is in the earth beneath, or that is in the water under the earth.*
>
> *—Exodus 20:4*

> *You shall not bow down to them nor serve them. For I, the LORD your God, am a jealous God, visiting the iniquity of the fathers upon the children to the third and fourth generations of those who hate Me.*
>
> *—Exodus 20:5*

Religions' gods are usually created or ordained (if it is a person) by men in order to deceive people to believe that such gods have powers. These gods are full of wicked spirits, and are controlled by demons. They are very dangerous and harmful, especially to those who do not believe or worship them. They are opposition to God and challenge His supernatural power. Many people worship and appeal to these ungodly gods without knowing the implication of what they are doing, and how perilous it is to worship these satanic gods. God commands us not to have anything to do with or worship any of these blasphemous and impious strange gods.

> *There shall be no foreign god among you; nor shall you worship any foreign god.*
> —*Psalms 81:9*

Other strange gods are witchcrafts, wizards, and witchdoctors. The people who revere or worship them believe they have power to kill human beings. If they have power to kill, such powers are limited when it comes to challenging the power of the Most High God. Witchcrafts, wizards, and witchdoctors are human beings who operate within the satanic realm, and they are full of evil spirits. Witchdoctors, for example, carve idols in form of a being or objects and invoke demons in them, and then worship them as their god. Many people believe that witchdoctors have the power to solve troubles and problems. They believe that witchdoctors can heal sick people and those who are carrying diseases. They believe that witchdoctors have the power to make people successful and rich. They also believe that witchdoctors have power to destroy and restore destinies and lives.

The other gods are those gods that our ancestors worshipped. Many families still worship these gods today, dedicating their children to these gods before and after their birth. This is a customary ceremony to show respect and recognition to their ancestors' gods. Those kids, who are dedicated to the gods, will be controlled by the gods when they grow up. In real life, these kids will struggle and find it difficult to live the life that God gives. They will behave strangely like those possessed with demonic spirits. However, they can only be free from such bondage if they receive spiritual deliverance. In addition, there are many people today who dedicate their marriage to the gods their fathers served. During the traditional marriage ceremony, they pour drinks on the ground and call the names of their ancestors and gods to complete the ceremony.

> *Now therefore, fear the Lord, serve Him in sincerity and in truth, and put away the gods, which your fathers served on the other side of the River and in Egypt. Serve the Lord!*
> —*Joshua 24:14*

The mermaid (water goddess) is another god worshipped by many people. Many countries worship the water goddess but in different ways. In some countries, when a woman has not conceived after been married for a long time, she will go to the river or beach to perform some rituals in the water. The ceremony is about appealing to the goddess and asking her for a child. The woman will make promise to dedicate the child to the goddess after birth. When the woman becomes pregnant and the child is born, another water ceremony is performed, and the baby will be given to the water goddess. The child will be possessed and manipulated by the mermaid spirits. Not all the children who have been dedicated to mermaid are aware of the agreement their mother and the water goddess have made concerning their lives. Some of these children grow up and get favoured in many ways (but it won't last); others will have difficulties succeeding in life. Such yoke will not be unyoked, except through prayer and fasting.

> *So He said to them, 'This kind can come out by nothing but prayer and fasting.'*
> —*Mark 9:29*

Religion can be practised in many ways, and many people practise it unknowingly. Some other examples of religion practicing are: putting your role models, idols, parents, or yourself before God; desiring men of God more than God; seeking men's approval rather than God's approval; honouring the elders (including village elders) instead of God; trying to please men instead of God; fearing the devil rather than God; spending more time with men of God than with God; denying that Jesus is the Son of God and God Himself; giving glory to men of God or their ministers' rather than exalting God; going to God through another source or human beings;, going to church on Sundays to fulfil tradition rather than to seek the face of God; relying on men (including men of God) rather than God; focusing on miracles rather than the Word of God, following traditions that are doctrines of men (including church traditions) rather than God's direction.

As there are too many religions, there are also too many false prophets. False prophets lie about many things; for example, they lie to people, claiming that God has told them that a man or woman is their spouse. The people they lie to will believe their prophecy and marry the wrong person, and as a result, they will experience problems later in their marriage. Sometimes these men and women who call themselves prophets engage themselves with evil activities, and they ask people to get involved, including those looking for someone to marry. They carry out their evil activities using the name of God so that people will think or believe they were sent by God.

> *I have not sent these prophets, yet they ran; I have not spoken to them, yet they prophesied.*
>
> *—Jeremiah 23:21*

> *I have heard what the prophets have said who prophesies lies in My name, saying, 'I have dreamed, I have dreamed!'*
>
> *—Jeremiah 23:25*

> *Thus says the Lord of hosts: Do not listen to the words of the prophets who prophesy to you. They make you worthless; they speak a vision of their own heart, not from the mouth of the Lord.*
>
> *—Jeremiah 23:16*

> *And we know that the Son of God has come and has given us an understanding, that we may know Him who is true; and we are in Him who is true, in His Son Jesus Christ. This is the true God and eternal life.*
>
> *—1 John 5:20*

Beware of false prophets, who come to you in sheep's clothing, but inwardly they are ravenous wolves.

—Matthew 7:15

You will know them by their fruits. Do men gather grapes from thorn bushes or figs from thistles?

—Matthew 7:16

Even so, every good tree bears good fruit, but a bad tree bears bad fruit.

—Matthew 7:17

A good tree cannot bear bad fruit, nor can a bad tree bear good fruit.

—Matthew 7:18

Every tree that does not bear good fruit is cut down and thrown into the fire.

—Matthew 7:19

Therefore by their fruits you will know them.

—Matthew 7:20

And have no fellowship with the unfruitful works of darkness, but rather expose them.

—Ephesians 5:11

Many people are confused about Christianity, and many think that Christianity is a religion. Is Christianity a religion? The simple answer is no—Christianity is not a religion but a revelation. It is the truth, not the untruth. It is life, not death. It is light, not darkness. It is nothing to do with idols or gods. Christianity is Christ alive in us. It is having relationship and fellowship with Christ. The word Christian means Christ-like—that is, behaving in the manner Jesus Christ taught us. God is not religious, and neither is He part of any religion. Religions are created by men and are created to challenge the supreme power of the Most High God. Religious people do not believe that Jesus Christ is the Son of God. Some people believe He is the Son of God but do not believe He is God Himself. Religious people say that Jesus was a prophet. Others call Him a man who never fulfilled God's purpose on the earth. God is not a man who practises religions. He did not create the religions of this world—man did, to satisfy his sense of right and wrong. Man is forever learning and will never come to the understanding of the truth.

> *Always learning, and never able to come to the knowledge of the truth.*
>
> *—2 Timothy 3:7*

> *Every spirit that does not confess that Jesus Christ has come in the flesh is not of God. And this is the spirit of the Antichrist, which you have heard was coming, and is now already in the world.*
>
> *—1 John 4:3*

Many times I have heard Christians say, 'It is one God, and therefore it does not matter.' The Christian God is different from Islamic, Hindu, Buddhism, and all religions' gods or idols. The Christian God is not described as an idol or god, and neither does He belong to any religious group. Many Christians have no true knowledge of the Word of God. Lack of knowledge is like a disease that destroys people. The religions' gods or idols are not real and cannot be compared to the Christian's Mighty God. Christians who do not study their Bible very well will never find out the truth. There is only one God and one mediator between God and men, Christ Jesus.

> *And you shall know the truth, and the truth shall make you free.*
>
> *—John 8:32*

> *For there is one God and one Mediator between God and men, the man Christ Jesus.*
>
> *—1 Timothy 2:5*

God is a loving God, and His love is flawless, immaculate, holy, and perpetual. God loves man unconditionally that He had to send His one precious Son to come into this world and save man. Jesus gave His life on the Cross of Calvary, shedding His blood to atone for sin. He brought life to man and made it possible for all men to be free from the penalty of sin, which is death or endless separation from Almighty God. God wants every person to have a good relationship with Him, and that is the reason why He gave the world His Son. Man can only have a good relationship with God through Christ, and no man can go to God except through Jesus. Those who have accepted Jesus are no longer condemned but are guaranteed to have an everlasting life. Jesus is the Light of the world, and those who follow Him shall have the light of life.

> *For God so loved the world that He gave His only begotten Son, that whoever believes in Him should not perish but have everlasting life.*
>
> *—John 3:16*

> *Jesus said to him, 'I am the way, the truth, and the life. No one comes to the Father except through Me.'*
>
> *—John 14:6*

> *He who believes in Him is not condemned; but he who does not believe is condemned already, because he has not believed in the name of the only begotten Son of God.*
>
> *—John 3:18*

> *He who believes in the Son has everlasting life; and he who does not believe the Son shall not see life, but the wrath of God abides on him.*
>
> *—John 3:36*

> *I am the Light of the world: He that follows me shall not walk in darkness, but shall have the light of life.*
>
> *—John 8:12*

Many Christians have asked whether it is wrong for a Christian to marry an unbeliever. The answer is yes, because unbelievers do not know God, and neither do they do His will. Therefore Christians must not associate with or befriend unbelievers. Christians also ought not to be unequally yoked with the unbelievers. In other words, believers should not be in the same level with the unbelievers or do what the unbelievers do or believe in their doctrines and false religions. Christians have nothing in common with the unbelievers. In spite of what the Word of God says concerning unbelievers, many Christians befriend unbelievers and embrace what they do. Some Christians marry unbelievers and think it is okay. When Christians marry non-Christians, they will not only experience problems in their relationship but also will have a marriage breakdown due to their life and marriage being controlled by religious spirits. The problem may not start at the early phases, but it will arise later in the marriage. The Christian spouse without doubt will struggle most in their relationship as he/ she tries to make it work. The more Christians try to make it work, the more they will get frustrated, because the couple has nothing in common (unless one spouse compromises, the marriage will not last).

> *Do not be unequally yoked together with unbelievers. For what fellowship has righteousness with lawlessness? And what communion has light with darkness?*
> —*2 Corinthians 6:14*

> *If we say that we have fellowship with Him, and walk in darkness, we lie and do not practice the truth.*
> —*1 John 1:6*

> *And if anyone does not obey our word in this epistle, note that person and do not keep company with him, that he may be ashamed.*
> —*2 Thessalonians 3:14*

Story 1

Mr S, an Islamic believer, got married to Mrs S, a Christian believer. Before they wed under Islamic law, Mr S promised Mrs S that he would allow her to continuing practising her Christian faith. After they got married, Mr S condemned Christianity and told her to practise the Islamic religion instead. Mrs S was given two choices: to remain in marriage (as a Muslim) or to leave their matrimonial home if she continued to worship Christ. Mrs S chose Islam and rejected Christianity. Her husband did not allow her and their children to watch Christian TV or to listen to Christian music. At the moment, Mrs S is struggling in their marriage and doing everything to make it work. She is not happy and sometimes gets frustrated.

Story 2

Mr and Mrs O were married for more than fourteen years before their marriage came to an end. Mrs O was a Christian before she met Mr O, a religious man attending the Grail Movement. Grail Movement members do not believe in God, and neither do they believe in the birth, death, and resurrection of Christ Jesus. They believe in plants and flowers, and they worship them as their gods. When Mrs O got married to Mr O, he stopped her from going to church, and she was converted to Grail Movement. They both had children together and dedicated all of them to the gods of Grail Movement society. Mrs O did everything in her power to make their relationship work, but it was not enough to keep their marriage alive.

A majority of Christians have asked how they can preach to unbelievers without being their friends first. Christians should love and pray for unbelievers but do not have to befriend them. God wants you to convert unbelievers but does not want religious people to convert you to their religion. When the Scripture says you should go into the world and preached the gospel, it did not say you should befriend unbelievers first before preaching the Word. Christians are born of God; unbelievers are not. Christians are the children of the Light (Christ) while the unbelievers belong to the dark. Darkness and light cannot walk together. Christians are the light of the world and therefore should not date or marry those who live in darkness.

One of the truest stories ever told is the story of Samson. Samson was the strongest man in the whole world. The Scripture said Samson went down to Timnath and saw a woman, the daughter of the Philistines. He went up and told his father and mother, 'I have seen a woman in Timnath of the daughters of the Philistines; now therefore, get her for me as a wife.' Then his father and mother said to him, 'Is there no woman among the daughters of your brethren, or among all my people, that you must go and get a wife from the uncircumcised Philistines?' Samson said to his father, 'Get her for me, for she pleases me well' (Judges 14:2-3).

The conflict between the Israelites and the Philistines started before the birth of Samson. The Israelites were not allowed to marry the Philistines, and the same was true of Philistines. If the Israelites and philistines do not give in marriage, why did Samson marry the daughter of the Philistines? Samson sought for the daughters of the Philistines because it was the will of God for him to marry the daughters of the Philistines. God allowed the marriage between Samson and Timnath to take place because the Philistines had dominion over the Israelites.

> *But his father and mother did not know that it was of the Lord that He was seeking an occasion to move against the Philistines. For at that time the Philistines had dominion over Israel.*
> —*Judges 14:4*

The birth of Samson was for a purpose. The purpose was to deliver the Israelites from their enemy, the Philistines. God knew that if Samson sought to marry from the Philistines, the Philistines would try to lay their hands on the Israelites, so He allowed it for His name to be glorified. The Almighty God wanted the Philistines to know that the God of Israel does not sleep.

> *Behold, He who keeps Israel shall neither slumber nor sleep.*
> —*Psalms 121:4*

If God chooses people for a mission, He has a purpose for that mission and will inform them on how to execute that mission. He will guide and protect them throughout the mission, to avoid the distraction and distraught of the enemy. There is no doubt that people will experience obstacles during the mission. However, if they obey the Word of God and work according to His will and directions, they will overcome every hindrance and obstacle. As for Samson, he was not aware of his purpose, and neither did he understand his mission. The enemy will always use someone very close. Samson should have learnt a lesson from his previous marriage, after he told his first wife his riddle and she revealed it to the children of her people.

> *Now she had wept on him the seven days while their feast lasted. And it happened on the seventh day that he told her, because she pressed him so much. Then she explained the riddle to the sons of her people.*
>
> —*Judges 14:17*

Afterwards, it came to pass that Samson loved a woman in the Valley of Sorek, whose name was Delilah. The lords of the Philistines came up to her and said to her, 'Entice him, and find out where his great strength lies, and by what means we may overpower him, that we may bind him to afflict him; and every one of us will give you eleven hundred pieces of silver' (Judges 16:4-5).

Delilah tried three times to know where Samson got his strength, and Samson lied to her. Samson did not learn a lesson from his previous marriage. When Samson lied to Delilah three times about where his strength came from, and she revealed it to the Philistines, Delilah's untrustworthy behaviour was enough for Samson to know the kind of person she was and what she was up to. But Samson did not perceive the cunning side of Delilah and later revealed the secret of his strength.

> *Delilah said to him: 'How can you say, "I love you," when your heart is not with me? You have mocked me these three times, and have not told me where your great strength lies.'*
>
> —*Judges 16:15*

> *That he told her all his heart, and said to her: 'No razor has ever come upon my head, for I have been a Nazirite to God from my*

> *mother's womb; If I am shaven, then my strength will leave me,*
> *and I shall become weak, and be like any other man.'*
>
> —*Judges 16:17*

Then Delilah lulled him to sleep on her knees and called for a man to shave off the seven locks of his head. Then she began to torment him, and his strength left him, (Judges 16:19).

> *The thief does not come except to steal, and to kill, and to*
> *destroy. I have come that they may have life, and that they may*
> *have it more abundantly.*
>
> —*John 10:10*

Samson knew he was extraordinary and knew where his strength came from; he knew what could happen to him if he revealed his strength, yet he disclosed it. When Samson revealed the secret of his strength, he voluntarily walked into the cage of Delilah, becoming his own enemy by allowing Delilah to convince him. Samson was manipulated and controlled by the spirit of self-destruction (religious spirit). Samson did not only contribute to his destruction but terminated his mission and destiny.

Many people are like Samson; they have helped their enemies to end their mission and destroy their lives. Today the majority of people are living with Delilah (the enemy). Christians should not bring in or associate with anything that the enemy can use to terminate their assignment or destiny. The Christians that I spoke to concerning their marriage to an unbeliever claimed it was God that chose their spouse. If it is true (but doubt it is) that God chose their non-belief spouse, He had a reason for it (and it will be for His name to be glorified). His motive must be to use those Christians to convert and bring salvation into the life of their unbelief spouse and his or her family. Christians who are married to unbelievers, and have not yet converted them or brought salvation to their lives, ought to know that their marriage is not destined by God.

The Philistines took Samson, put out his eyes, and brought him down to Gaza. They bound him with bronze fetters, and he became a grinder in the prison (Judges 16:21). This was not what God wished for Samson, and neither was it the way God planned it. Samson was a man born to be warrior. His was a man called to deliver his people, the Israelites. It was not the will of God for Samson to end in the hands of the Philistines. If God calls someone for a mission, He wants them to complete that mission, and would not want them to end their assignment or calling in a shameful way. Samson did not complete his mission—he chose to please Delilah instead of God. He was pleasing the devil, and never knew he was selling the secret of his strength. God departed from Samson when he allowed the enemy to take over his life and end his destiny.

> *And Delilah said, 'The Philistines are upon you, Samson!' So he awoke from his sleep, and said, 'I will go out as before, at other times, and shake myself free!' But he did not know that the Lord had departed from him.*
>
>   *—Judges 16:20*

Many spouses are in trouble because the enemy has taken control of their marriage. When the enemy takes control of a relationship, God departs. The story of Samson is a good example of how the enemy can easily end missions, marriages, and even lives through religious spirits. Samson knew he was unique, chosen by God from birth. He also recognised he was different from others because of his strange strength. However, what he did not know was that God selected him for a special task: to deliver the Israelites. He was too ignorant to know that he was not supposed to reveal the secret of his strength. As this was not part of his calling, God departed from him, and he lost his strength to the enemy.

> *My people are destroyed for lack of knowledge: Because you have rejected knowledge, I also will reject you from being priest for Me: Because you have forgotten the law of your God, I also will forget your children.*
>
>   *—Hosea 4:6*

COUNSEL

There are many gods or idols, but there is only one God. Anybody or anything can be gods or idols, but nobody or anything can be Almighty God. The existence of God cannot be questioned, and neither can His Words be questioned because they are binding and will remain forever. God cannot go against His Words. His Words are strict and must be obeyed. Do not be deceived, for God is not a god, and He did not establish the religion of this world; men did to satisfy their self-interest. God is a jealous God. Do not worship any other god except Him. Once again, there is only one true God, and you cannot go to Him unless you go through Jesus. Therefore if you do not worship Jesus, you do not worship God.

> Jesus said to him, 'I am the way, the truth, and the life. No one comes to the Father except through Me.'
> —*John 14:6*

> All should honour the Son just as they honour the Father. He who does not honour the Son does not honour the Father who sent Him.
> —*John 5:23*

The Word of God says, 'Beloved, believe not every spirit, but try the spirits whether they are of God: because many false prophets are gone out into the world' (1 John 4:1). In other words, you should not believe every prophecy but must first test the spirit that is in the person prophesying to you, to know if the spirit in him/her is of God. But how can you know the Spirit that is in a prophet or whether a prophecy is actually from God? The answer is that you must accept Jesus as your one and only Saviour, you must receive the Holy Spirit, and you must worship God in truth and in spirit. If you have no advice from the Spirit of God, there is no way you would know a prophecy that is not of God. As I said earlier in the chapter; false prophets lie to and deceive people that God said that a man or woman is their chosen spouse. God can reveal your spouse through men of God, but be careful because not all prophecies are from God. When you hear from a man of God that a person is your future spouse, do not rush into marriage immediately, but pray and wait until God confirms the prophecy to you. God will also reveal the same prophecy to that man or woman He has chosen for you, and possibly revealed it to some brethrens (not *necessary from the church you attend). God is never confused, so He will not put you in a state of disorder. Furthermore, God can reveal something alone to one person, if he does not want others to know about it. However, when it comes to relationships, God will reveal to more than one person. Therefore when a prophet tells you that a particular person is your spouse, and that the prophecy is from God, go to God in prayer and ask Him to reveal it to you.*

Story 3

A lady and a man hardly knew each other. They got together and did a traditional wedding. After their traditional wedding they moved in together and had more than three children. According to them, they were born-again Christians and still had not bothered to wed in the church. Before they met each other, the man used to go to church, but since they started living together, he stopped going. The man did not desire to wed in the church, and neither was he interested in practising Christianity. Once he returned to work, he run straight to his computer. They don't spend time with each other; all they do is argue, and there is no taste of love in their relationship. They have no passion or love for each other. The lady complained about their relationship not working and said that she would like to separate from the man. During our conversation, I found out that the man had previously married and divorced. She said a man of God told her that God said that the man was her husband. I felt sorry for her and said to her that the man was not chosen by God but by the man of God. I said to her that the blessings of the Lord makes us rich and causes no sorrows and it is wrong to marry a divorcee.

> *The blessing of the LORD makes* one *rich, and He adds no sorrow with it.*
> —*Proverbs 10:22*

> *Whoever marries a divorcee commits adultery.*
> —*Matthew 5:32b*

A majority of Christians do not understand the difference between traditional wedding and church wedding. Traditional weddings are different from holy weddings (church weddings). Traditional weddings were established by the ancestors. A traditional wedding is not divine, and it is done to fulfil the tribe or village custom. A traditional marriage is a choice; you are not bound to perform such a ceremony. Believers who do it do not follow their future spouse home until after they have completed their holy wedding. It is the unbelievers (whether a Christian or not) that follow their future spouse home and start cohabiting. A true believer will never forget to wed in the church and receive blessings from God. You must wed in the church because it is a must and not by choice.

Once more, Christianity means having fellowship with Christ. The word Christian means Christ-like. If your behaviour or character is like Christ, you are indeed a true Christian. If you do not portray the image of Christ, you are an unbeliever. It does not matter that you have confessed your sins and said the acceptance words, but; if your conduct is outside the Word of God, you are certainly not a believer. In addition, if you were born and raised in the church; you are not a good Christian unless you have received Christ. The fact that you go to church every Sunday does not make you a good Christian. A Christian must be a practising Christian to be regarded as a good Christian. A good Christian does not nail Christ twice on the cross. A good Christian carries the cross and follows Christ. A good Christian always does the will of the Heavenly Father.

By now, you must know that Christianity is not a religion. Therefore do not desire to associate with religious people or do what they do. Do not marry anyone who is not a Christian. Do not marry a religious person (an unbeliever), even if you think you can make them become a Christian. Do not marry an unbeliever or religious person, even if he/she promises to allow you to go to church or continue practising Christianity. Christians be wise, and do not be deluded by unbelievers; put your trust in God alone.

There are differences between Christians and non-Christians. First, Christians are believers while non-Christians are unbelievers (whether religious or atheist). A believer seeks the face of God at all times; an unbeliever does not seek the face of God but does what he likes as long as it pleases him. A believer seeks God's approval before doing things, while an unbeliever does things without seeking God's approval. A believer focuses on the Most High God, but an unbeliever focuses on the things of the world and the demons that control him. A believer exalts God, while an unbeliever exalts gods, demons,

Satan, religions, mermaids, witches, humans, wizards, idols, and everything contrary to the Word of God. A believer would rather marry a believer than an unbeliever, whereas an unbeliever marries anyone (to them all religions are the same). A believer does not practise religion, but an unbeliever does. A believer first goes to God in prayer for confirmation (when it comes to selecting a spouse), but an unbeliever does not think it is necessary to verify with God. A believer does not see Christianity as a religion, while an unbeliever sees it as a religion. A believer fears God, whereas an unbeliever fears man and the devil. A believer inquires from God before doing things, whereas an unbeliever does things without enquiring from God. A believer does the will of God, while an unbeliever does the will of man. A believer praises God, while unbeliever praises man. A believer has hope in God, whereas an unbeliever puts faith and trust in man. A believer spends more time with God rather than men of God; an unbeliever seeks to know men of God more than God (they prefer miracles and blessings over God Himself). A believer seeks to know Jesus Christ and desires to have a good relationship with Him; an unbeliever desires to know the world and associates with other unbelievers. A believer knows that Jesus is the Christ but an unbeliever denies that Jesus is the Christ.

> *Who is a liar but he who denies that Jesus is the Christ? He is antichrist who denies the Father and the Son.*
>
> —*1 John 2:22*

> *Whoever denies the Son does not have the Father either; he who acknowledges the Son has the Father also.*
>
> —*1 John 2:23*

Story 4

I met a woman, and when I started to chat with her, I found out that she was cohabiting with a Muslim man. She already had a child with the man, and they were planning for a second baby. I spoke to her concerning her relationship with the Islamic man. She told me she was a born-again and that she worshipped at a well-known Pentecostal church. When I tried to make her see sense, she said to me, 'It does not matter; there is nothing wrong with dating an unbeliever. Everyone in the church knows about my relationship with the Muslim man, and they are cool about it.' She also said they were planning for their wedding. I was shocked and surprised! I asked myself where they would be getting married, in the church or a mosque. The answer was—mosque of course, because no Muslim man would want to wed in the church. It is unbelievable and awful that a Christian who called herself a believer and worshipped in a Pentecostal church would choose to go the wrong route because everybody in her place of worship embraces her ungodly relationship.

This is absolutely wrong! Do not be ignorant of the Word. Have you forgotten that believers have nothing in common with unbelievers? Do you not know that believers must not associate with unbelievers? What friendship has righteousness with iniquity, or what understanding has light with darkness? What unity has Christ with Belial? What has a believer in common with an unbeliever? What agreement has the temple of God with idols? Christians are the temple of the living God, as God said, 'He will live in them and move among them, He will be their God, and they shall be His people. Therefore, Christians must separate from Non-Christians, says the Lord, and touch nothing unclean, so that God will welcome them, and be a father to them, and they shall be His sons and daughters, says the Lord Almighty.'

> Do not be unequally yoked together with unbelievers. For what fellowship has righteousness with lawlessness? And what communion has light with darkness?
> —2 Corinthians 6:14

> And what accord has Christ with Belial? Or what part has a believer with an unbeliever?
> —2 Corinthians 6:15

> And what agreement has the temple of God with idols? For you are the temple of the living God, as God has said: I will dwell in them, and walk among them. I will be their God, and they shall be My people.
> —2 Corinthians 6:16

> Come out from among them, and be separate, says the Lord. Do not touch what is unclean, and I will receive you.
> —2 Corinthians 6:17

*I will be a Father to you, and you shall be My sons and daughters
says the Lord Almighty.*

　　　　　　　　　　　　　　—2 Corinthians 6:18

*Darkness and light cannot walk together! You are either of Christ or the devil!
A minister of God who cares only about big congregations, money, and miracles
is making a huge error. As a man of God, your main focus should be preaching
the salvation of Christ, teaching people how to have a good relationship with
God, and ensuring that the Word of God is truthfully and precisely preached
and taught. The devil is after the children of God, and he is doing everything in
his power to destroy their marriages and lives through sin and religious spirits.
He has taken control of some ministries and their congregations; some Churches
cannot see it because they are too busy competing with one another.*

*Many Christians are living an impious life, not knowing that what they are
doing is wrong because no ministers warn them. It is not surprising because
there are many divorced ministers, and they hardly condemn divorce. God has
not placed ministers in ministries to focus on their own interests but to speak
the truth about morals, salvation, and the second coming of Christ. God is not
happy about what is happening in churches today. Though many ministers
have performed great miracles, perhaps even greater miracles than Christ, the
Scripture says on the last day, God will reject those who did not do His will
or obey the Word of God.*

> *Many will say to Me in that day, 'Lord, Lord, have we not
> prophesied in Your name, cast out demons in Your name, and
> done many wonders in Your name?'*
> 　　　　　　　　　　　　　　*—Mathew 7:22*

> *And then I will declare to them, 'I never knew you; depart from
> Me, you who practice lawlessness!'*
> 　　　　　　　　　　　　　　*—Matthew 7:23*

> *But if they had stood in my counsel, and had caused my people
> to hear my words, then they would have turned them from their
> evil way, and from the evil of their doings.*
> 　　　　　　　　　　　　　　*—Jeremiah 23:22*

There is no doubt that many people, including Christians, do not know how dangerous the spirits that control religions are and how they operate within humans. It is very important that every Christian be aware of how religious spirits work and how they control people's lives. These are some of the things you should know about religious spirits.

Religious spirits are full of heaviness; this is the time when you feel heaviness around you because of certain people or surroundings. It is the time when you are unable to pray because of the atmosphere of the place where you are. It is the time when you get upset and find it difficult to pray because you are not happy with the way things are going for you. It is the time when you woke up in the morning and felt sad and unhappy for no reason. It is also the time when you were spiritually attacked by anti-prayer spirits. It is the time when you felt depressed and did not want anyone around you, because you wanted to be on your own.

Religious spirits are attackers; they attack believers because of the image they represent. The attack could be physical or spiritual.

- *Physical:* It the time when you experienced hatred from co-workers; no matter what you do, they don't seem to like you. It is the time when you cannot talk to people because you fear if you do, they might argue with you or even say things that upset you. It is also the time when you have been hit by someone for no reason.

- *Spiritual:* this is the time when you are unable to pray or call the blood or name of Jesus because you've been oppressed or attacked by someone or something in your dream. It is the time when you have dreams and see yourself chased by unknown or known people. It is the time when you dream of snakes or dogs running after you or barking at you or even biting you. If you see yourself being accused in the dream, it is spiritual attack, and it is caused by religious spirits.

Religious spirits are controllers; this is the time when you feel that you cannot express yourself because you do not want to offend a person of another belief. It is the time when you did things that your mates or spouse asked you to do, and you knew it was not right but did it because you did not want them to hate you. It is when people (whether a believer or unbeliever) are controlled and manipulated, and they do something which they later regret; for example, many couples who killed their spouses did show remorse and claimed that they did not know what was controlling them. It is also the time when you found it hard to stop something which you knew was wrong because you were addicted to it. It is when a wife refuses to submit to her husband because she feels superior to him. It is when a wife controls her husband or sees herself as the head of the family because she is the breadwinner of the family. It is when a married man still serves their siblings or parents because they are richer than him. Religious spirits are the cause of the warfare you face daily in your marriage.

Religious spirits are confusing spirits; this is when believers evangelise the Gospel of Christ and those they preach to, and the unbelievers come up with a question to confuse them. It is when individuals do not know want to believe anymore because of too many religions and doctrines. It is when people do something that is not right, but they convinced themselves it is okay because other people are doing it. It is the time when mothers believed that their children's bad behaviours were right because they were convinced that other kids behaved in the same manner. It is also when pastors who preach against something indirectly allow it in their ministry. It is when believers start to backslide because of a man of God's conduct.

Story 5

There was a man of God who established a ministry with the permission of a general overseer. One morning, according to him, he said that God wanted him to have his own ministry, and he told the general overseer and later the Church. He then came up with a new name for the ministry and scrapped the old name. Some of his congregation were unhappy and furious about the change. The following Sunday, half of the congregation left the ministry. There was a woman who was not in the church when the announcement was made; when she heard about it, she stopped going to church entirely, and remains at home every Sunday.

The story above shows that some people go to church because of man. Why should a Christian go to church because of their general overseer? A true Christian goes to church because they want to seek the face of God. The name *of the ministry was changed, not the name of God. It was the same man of God they had known for years; nothing changed. The congregation's action proves that they have no relationship with God, that all the time they were in that ministry they were worshipping the general overseer and not the Heavenly Father.*

Religious spirits are provoking spirits; this is when God has been criticised and challenged by the enemy or religious people. It is when non-Christians have said to believers that the God they serve is powerless. It is also when a believer has been challenged and questioned about the existence of God. It is the time when people criticised you for being a good Christian. It is when you are have been laughed at by people because you are suffering or going through hard times. It is the time when people laughed at you because you fasted and prayed but had not yet received your breakthrough. It is time when someone had said to you, 'If your God is a true God, why are you not successful?'

Religious spirits lure people into sexual acts; this is when people see themselves in a dream having romance or sex with someone they know or do not know. It is the time when people are interested in sexual acts or inducing someone into it. It is the time when a person seduced someone to fall for him/her sexually. It is the time when people abused themselves sexually. It when people engaged in prostitution, using it as a business. It is the time when a man or woman sleeps with a prostitute. It is when people have interest in things like lap dancing. It is when men admire or prefer to sleep with men. It is when women admire or prefer to sleep with women. It is the time when people abused children sexually. It is the time when people possess indecent images from the Internet. It is the time when fathers slept with their own children or touched them sexually. It is the time when Christian ministers had sexual relationships with their secretaries or congregation. It is the time when a pastor slept with prostitute or strange woman. It is the time when people used their spouse as a sex object or used force, threats, or intimidation to make them perform sexual acts. It is when people take pleasure in seeing naked women or men. It is when people enjoy reading books and magazines that contain porn or find interest in watching sexual and pornography films.

Story 6

There was a minister of God who had interest in pornography. He enjoyed reading books and magazines that contain naked women. He was married and was born again at the time he was tormented by religious spirits. According to his wife, he knew what he was doing was wrong but had no self-control. His wife said he would go inside his car and read pornography magazines or anything that had naked women in it. He was so obsessed with naked women and found pleasure from it. One day, he told his wife what had been happening to him. His wife took him to church counsellors, they counselled him, and he was delivered from God.

> *He who covers his sins shall not prosper, but whoever confesses and forsakes them will have mercy*
> —*Proverbs 28:13*

Religious spirits are full of lying spirits; this is the time when religious people or unbelievers have said to you, 'It does not matter, Christianity is the same as all religions.' It is the time when people accused you of blasphemy because they cannot stand the truth and the Spirit of God in you. It is when a member of your family has lied against you or accused you of doing something wrong because they want to embarrass you. It is the time when believers hear a voice that says to them, 'If Christ is real, why did he allow bereavement in your family?' It is when single people, trusting God for a spouse, are laughed at, tempted, and asked where their God is. It is the time when married people, believing God for the fruit of the womb, have been mocked and asked if their God is asleep. It is the time when a person has been told that sex before marriage is acceptable. It is when Christians are told that having sex with the same gender (homosexual and bisexual) is acceptable in the eyes of God. It is the time when married people are made to believe by their pastors that divorce is not a sin, and they can divorce their spouse on certain grounds. There are no grounds for divorce as spouses are under obligation to forgive their spouse for each sin they committed against them, including adultery.

> *Then Peter came to Him and said, 'Lord, how often shall my brother sin against me, and I forgive him? Up to seven times?'*
> —*Matthew 18:21*

Jesus said to him, 'I do not say to you, up to seven times, but up to seventy times seven.'

—*Matthew 18:22*

For whoever shall keep the whole law, and yet stumble in one point, he is guilty of all.

—*James 2:10*

The spirits that control religions are very dangerous, toxic, and deadly. They do not care who they destroy or kill. They are full of deceit and can easily convince people to believe their lies. Religious spirits turn families against one another and cause turmoil. They hate peace and create division. They are not reliable and cannot be trusted. They steal and have no compassion for anyone (including those who obey them). Religious spirits make people to do bad things, but when the worst comes, they reject them and leave them to die.

Story 7

There was a Christian couple who had been married for many years without children. The husband and wife both were believers and had prayed to God for a marriage reward. The woman went to different churches, but none was able to help her. She was criticised by her unbelieving in-laws for not having any kids. Her in-laws called her a man and told her to leave their son. They begged their son to divorce her and marry another woman. The only person on her side was her husband, who refused to listen to his parents.

One day, she met a true man of God and told her story. The man of God told her that she was unable to have children because of her father in-law. The woman told her in-laws that it was her father in-law who caused her barrenness, but no one believed her, including her husband. She fasted and prayed earnestly, and God answered her. She got pregnant, and her father in-law was admitted to the hospital. When she heard that her father-in-law was seriously ill, she went to the hospital to see him. When she saw her father-in-law, she urged him to confess. Her father-in-law told her that he joined an occult society because he wanted to live longer. He told her that he closed her womb so that he could live and not die. Nevertheless, the man died because he was unable to recover from his illness.

There is a way that seems right to a man but its end is the way of death.

—Proverbs 14:12

Religious spirits are demons, evil spirits. They are enemies to God, and they challenge Him and the Word of God. They also challenge His supernatural powers. Religious spirits deny that Jesus Christ is come in the fresh. Religious spirits deny that Christ is the Son of God. Religious spirits deny that Jesus Christ is God.

For unto us a Child is born, unto us a Son is given; and the government will be upon His shoulder. And His name will be called Wonderful, Counsellor, Mighty God, Everlasting Father, and Prince of Peace.

—Isaiah 9:6

In the beginning was the Word, and the Word was with God, and the Word was God.

—John 1:1

And the Word became flesh and dwelt (lived) among us.

—John 1:14

By this you know the Spirit of God: Every spirit that confesses that Jesus Christ has come in the flesh is of God.

—1 John 4:2

For many deceivers have gone out into the world, who do not confess that Jesus coming in the flesh. This is a deceiver and an antichrist.

—2 John 1:7

For God so loved the world that He gave His only begotten Son that whoever believes in Him should not perish but have everlasting life.

—John 3:16

Nine

Domestic Violence

IX

Domestic Violence

Domestic Violence is any incident of threatening behaviour, violence, or abuse (psychological, physical, sexual, or emotional) between adults who are or have been in a relationship, or between family members. It can affect anybody regardless of gender or sexuality. The violence used by men against their wives ranges across a very wide spectrum, from pushing and slapping to homicide. In a given relationship, the frequency of violent events may be regular and as frequent as several times a week or irregular and as infrequent as once a year. The consequences of the violence usually include physical injuries and negative emotional or psychological effects.

Domestic violence often escalates from threats and verbal abuse to violence. Whereas physical injury may be the most obvious danger, the emotional or psychological consequences of domestic abuse are also severe. Emotionally abusive relationships can destroy your self-worth, lead to anxiety and depression, and make you feel helpless and alone. No one should have to endure this kind of pain, and your first step to breaking free is recognising that your situation is abusive. Once you acknowledge the reality of the abusive situation, then you can get the help you need.

Domestic violence can happen to anyone, yet the problem is often overlooked, excused, or denied. No one should live in fear of the person they love. If you recognise yourself or someone you know in the following signs, do not hesitate to stop it. The signs of domestic violence are as follows:

- Destructive criticism and verbal abuse: shouting, mocking, accusing, swearing, and calling you names.

- Pressure tactics: sulking, threatening to withhold money; threatening to restrain you from moving or leaving the room; forcing you to do something against your will; threatening to disconnect the telephone; threatening to take the car away; threatening to commit suicide; threatening to kill you; threatening to take the children or report you to the welfare agencies.

- Physical attack: slapping or punching you on the face, body, arms or legs; pushing, grabbing or shoving you; using an object to harm you; kicking or punching you in the stomach when pregnant; trying to strangle, smother, or drown you; twisting your arm; dragging you or pulling you by the hair; choking you; holding your hands over your head or throwing things at you.

- Breaking trust: lying to you, withholding information from you, being jealous, having other relationships, breaking promises and shared agreements.

- Isolation: monitoring or blocking your telephone calls, telling you where you can and cannot go, preventing you from seeing friends and relatives.

- Harassment: following you, checking up on you, opening your mail, repeatedly checking to see who has telephoned you, embarrassing you in public.

- Threats: making angry gestures, using physical size to intimidate, shouting you down, destroying your possessions, breaking things, punching walls, wielding a knife or a gun, threatening to harm you and the children.

- Sexual violence: using force, threats, or intimidation to make you perform sexual acts; having sex with you when you don't want to have sex; any degrading treatment based on your sexual orientation.

- Denial: saying the abuse doesn't happen, saying you caused the abusive behaviour, being publicly gentle and patient, crying and begging for forgiveness, saying it will never happen again.

Here are some other signs of domestic violence.

- *You feel afraid of your spouse much of the time, avoid certain topics out of fear of angering your spouse, feel that you cannot do anything right for your spouse, believe that you deserve to be hurt or mistreated, wonder if you are the one who is crazy, feel emotionally numb or helpless.*

- *Your spouse humiliates or yells at you, criticizes you and put you down, treats you so badly that you are embarrassed for your friends or family to see, ignores or puts down your opinions or accomplishments, blames you for the abusive behaviour, sees you as property or a sex object rather than as a person.*

- *Your spouse has a bad and unpredictable temper, hurt you or threaten to hurt or kill you if you try to take your children away, threatens to commit suicide if you leave, forces you to have sex.*

- *Your spouse acts excessively jealous and possessive, controls where you go or what you do, keeps you from seeing your friends or family, limits your access to money, the phone, or the car.*

Story 1

Whilst at my previous employment, a man came into the office unhappy, confused, and emotionally distressed. When I spoke to him, I realised he was homeless. I referred him to one of my colleagues who deals with homelessness issues. After seeing my colleague, he was still angry. I called him and asked what the matter was, and he told me he did not get the help he came for. He said he was homeless because he had an argument with his wife, and she kicked him out of their home. He also said that for the past few months he had been a victim of domestic violent. He told me he had had enough and would file for divorce. I asked him if he was a Christian, and he said yes. I asked him what he thought God would want him to do in such a situation. He said he did not care, and as far as he was concerned, that their marriage was over. He told me he had a month-old baby, and his wife had not allowed him to see it. I advised him not to divorce his wife but to go home and pray. He left the office, and I committed the situation into the hands of God. Three weeks later he returned to the office to thank me for what God had done for him. This time he was so happy and looked peaceful that I did not recognise him until he made himself known to me. He told me that he took my advice and returned back to his wife and children.

It takes the Grace of God to do the right thing. When people obey the Word of God, He answers them. God is not a violent God, and therefore He cannot give you a violent spouse. When you find a spouse, the first thing you should do is to hand him/her over to God. The second thing is to take your spouse to church to hear the Word of God, as faith comes by hearing the Word.

> So then faith comes by hearing, and hearing by the Word of God.
>
> —Romans 10:17

Marriage problems do not always start as a result of husband's ill behaviour towards the wife. It could start once the man begins to listen to third parties and takes advice from them. When it comes to marriage or family matters, not everyone is qualified to give marital advice. Many problems that couples face within their marriage could have been resolved amicably if the couples had not taken their problems to the wrong people. Some couples sometimes take their marriage problems to those who were never their fans from day one. They rely on them to give them advice, when they should have known that such people could worsen their marital issues.

Story 2

Mr P and Ms J had lived together as married couple for seventeen years, and they had three children. Mr P was a business man and Ms J was a housewife. Mr P was the breadwinner of the family. Ms J was not able to work because her husband did not want her to work; she was responsible for domestic work and for taking care of the kids. Ms P and J's relationship was very good—until he started to have an affair with one of his customers. Mr P later became violent towards his wife and kids. He beat his wife as well as his children. His girlfriend advised him to leave his family when he told her that he was having problems with his wife. Mr P took his girlfriend's advice and left his wife and kids to live with his girlfriend. Ms J had no choice but to look for work. Family and friends (including Mr P's colleagues) were not happy with Mr P's decision. Mr P got depressed at work and later resigned. He turned his anger to his girlfriend, battered her, and left her with scars. After his girlfriend pressed charges against him, his eyes opened, and he acknowledged he had a problem. In order to make things right with Ms J and the children, Mr P sought help. He got the help he needed and went back and reconciled with his wife and children.

> *Do not be deceived: evil communications corrupt good manner.*
>
> > *1 Corinthians 15:33*

> *Awake to righteousness, and do not sin; for some do not have the knowledge of God. I speak this to your shame.*
>
> > *—1 Corinthians 15:34*

> *Ask, and it will be given to you; seek, and you will find; knock, and it will be opened to you.*
>
> > *—Matthew 7:7*

Story 3

Mr P and Ms M got married, and Mr P left the country to live and work in Europe. Mr P later brought his wife to Europe. According to Ms M, before she arrived in Europe, her husband promised to bring her there to live a better life. However, since Ms M arrived in Europe, Mr P had not allowed her to go out or visit places. She was restricted from associating with friends she already knew in her country of origin. Mr P never left her alone in the house because he did not trust her. Each time they went out, Mr P would leave Ms M and return home. Ms M, who was new in Europe, would borrow money from strangers to return home. One day, Mr P threatened to throw her out of the flat where they were living. She was repeatedly beaten by Mr P, and he also called her names. Mr P refused to allow her to go to college, which he had promised her before she came to Europe. His reason was that Ms M was too old to go to school. When Ms M became pregnant and had a boy, she thought having a child would change Mr P and stop him from abusing her. But the violent did not stop and went from bad to worse. Ms M was like a servant to Mr P and was never cared for. Mr P later told Ms M to either commit suicide or divorce him. When Mr P realised that Ms M won't commit suicide or divorce him, he moved out of the flat.

> Yet you say, 'For what reason?' Because the Lord has been witness between you and the wife of your youth, with whom you have dealt treacherously; yet she is your companion and your wife by covenant.
>
> —Malachi 2:14

> But did He not make them one, having a remnant of the Spirit? And why one? He seeks godly offspring. Therefore take heed to your spirit, and let none deal treacherously with the wife of his youth.
>
> —Malachi 2:15

For the Lord God of Israel says that He hates divorce, for it covers one's garment with violence, says the Lord of hosts. Therefore, take heed to your spirit that you do not deal treacherously.
—*Malachi 2:16*

Ms M's story is not the first time that has happened to a woman. Most men travel with their wives to foreign countries and behave spitefully towards them. However, women who experience this kind of maltreatment from their husbands are commonly women from black and ethnic minorities. These women may be particularly inhibited from reporting domestic violence because of the provisions of immigration legislation. The women involved are likely to be apprehensive about using the legal justice system because they realise that they are in peril of being forced to leave the country, and they believe that the authorities will take action against them.

Story 4

Ms V was seventeen when she met Mr T, and they had a very serious relationship. Ms V had a sensible job and was living happily with her parents. Ms V described Mr T as having an irresistible, bad-boy appeal. Mr T showered Ms V with gifts and compliments, and Ms V left her job and parents to live with him in another city. One day, Mr T and Ms V were in Mr T's parents' house. Mr T became annoyed and behaved aggressively towards her when she mentioned her plan to visit her sister. Ms V ran out of the house, and Mr T ran after her and threatened to hit her with a table leg.

When things settled down between them, Ms V left Mr T to live with her sister. One night, Ms V and her sister were having a barbecue party. Mr T showed up and was wearing a bullet-proof vest. He had a bottle of brandy in one hand and a knife in the other. When Ms V called the police, Mr T threatened to hurt her if she allowed the police inside the house. Ms V's sister told the police it was a false alarm, and the police left. Afterwards Mr T left Ms V's sister house and never returned.

When Ms V thought she had finally got her life back, Mr T appeared when she was waiting for a bus, and he pulled her inside a vehicle and drove away. They got to a place where no one was around, and Mr T punched her in the face. Mr T ripped her top and bra off and put his hands around her neck. Ms V shouted but no one could hear her. She was repeatedly beaten and hit with a metal bar. She blacked out and was left to die. When Ms V was found, she was taken to the hospital. The doctor who treated her said if she had not been brought to the hospital she would have died. The police later caught Mr T, and he was convicted. He is currently serving a long sentence.

> *There is a way* that seems *right to a man but its end* is *the way of death.*
>
> —*Proverbs 14:12*

Although hitting, slapping, and kicking are the most common forms of physical attack, unnatural sex is also a domestic violence and is commonly used to abuse women. Sexual assault in intimate relationships is thought to be widespread, and it includes forced sex, the use of implements in assaulting the partner sexually, urinating on the partner, tying up the partner, forcing the partner to mimic or take part in pornography, and forcing the person to take part in sexual acts with acquaintances.

Story 5

Years ago, a man came back from work and told his wife that he was going to a pub to drink. His wife responded, 'Be careful because you have not had anything to eat, and your dinner will be ready by evening.' The man returned home at midnight and was really drunk. He forced his wife to have sex because he was out of his mind. His wife fought back, but he violently pushed his way through her defences, hitting her the entire time.

COUNSEL

Your spouse is a victim of domestic violence if you mock, shout, accuse, verbally threaten, or call him/her names. Your spouse is a victim of domestic violence if you are monitoring or blocking his or her telephone calls, telling them where they can and cannot go, or preventing them from seeing friends and relatives. You are an abuser if you use force, threaten, or intimidate to make your spouse perform sexual acts, or if you have sex with your spouse when he/she does not want to have sex.

Domestic violence is one of the offensive weapons that the devil uses to destroy marriages. Domestic violence does not only destroy marriages, it also ruins the lives of the couples involved. The spouses who experience domestic violence sometimes do not know that they have been victims of such aggression. They think it is one of those behaviours that they have to put up with in marriage. Domestic violence is a brutal behaviour, and spouses should not tolerate such conduct.

If you are not sure whether you are or have been a victim of domestic violence, read this chapter carefully again so that you will be aware of the signs of domestic violence and how offensive it is. Domestic violence is a serious offence because it is wrongful to be violent, and it is dangerous to put up with violent behaviour. Many people have died because of domestic violence they suffered in their homes. Do not ignore violence if you experience it in your marriage—seek help immediately if you notice the signs of domestic violence. There are good churches around you where you can make reports concerning your spouse's behaviour towards you. Ensure that prayers are conducted daily for you and your spouse, and if possible, pray and fast for your spouse to be delivered. Remember, there are things that cannot be solved except by praying and fasting. Moreover, the Scripture says that with God, all things are possible.

> *So He said to them, 'This kind can come out by nothing but prayer and fasting.'*
> —Mark 9:29

> *But Jesus looked at them and said to them, 'With men this is impossible, but with God all things are possible.'*
> —Matthew 19: 26

The reason some spouses act violently towards their spouse is because they have no fear of God. True believers cannot be violent towards their spouse because they have fear and respect for God Almighty. Unbelievers are the only people who treat their spouses treacherously. This is why it is important that you marry a believer—that is, a born-again Christian—so that you can experience the best that God gives in marriage. You should not argue or fight with your spouse at all times. Marriage is all about love, care, excitement, enjoyment, friendship, pleasure, peace, and happiness.

Spouses, who act violently towards their spouse, are mostly those who did not have a good upbringing. Some of them were brought up by violent and abused parents, while some were not but act violently because they are insecure. No matter what your upbringing or experience as a child, you should not abuse your spouse. You should let the past stay in the past—do not take it with you to your matrimonial home. Those who fight their spouse are not doing the will of God but the will of the devil.

To follow in the footsteps of your parents is not always the best idea. Let your behaviour be that of Christ, gentle and meek in heart. Try to give love to your new family because it will make your marriage successful and stronger. Leave behind those things that make you behave ungodly towards your spouse and embrace the joy that God has given to both of you. Domestic violence is the acts of unrighteous people. Those who abuse (verbally or physically) or act violently towards their spouse will not enter the Kingdom of God.

> *Do you not know that the unrighteous will not inherit the kingdom of God? Do not be deceived. Neither fornicators, nor idolaters, nor adulterers, nor homosexuals, nor sodomites;*
> *—1 Corinthians 6:9*

> *Nor thieves, nor covetous, nor drunkards, nor revilers, nor extortioners will inherit the kingdom of God.*
> *—1 Corinthians 6:10*

An act of domestic violent is committed as a result of anger. If you are an angry person, it proves you have the spirit of anger. The spirit of anger is of the devil, and to be angry to an extent that you can no longer control it is a sin. Those who are easily provoked are the people who have submitted to the spirit of anger. Such people find it difficult to forgive and will never be happy until they have caused injury. If you are unable to forgive someone, God will not forgive your trespasses.

> And whenever you stand praying, if you have anything against anyone, forgive him that your Father in heaven may also forgive you your trespasses.
> —Mark 11:25

> And forgive us our debts, as we forgive our debtors.
> —Matthew 6:12

> Bearing with one another, and forgiving one another, if anyone has a complaint against another; even as Christ forgave you, so you also must do.
> —Colossians 3:13

If you want to build a good matrimonial relationship, you must have self-control. When you are offended by your spouse, make it known to your spouse and expect an apology from them. If your spouse is the type that is too proud or always claims to be right even when he is wrong, try to avoid talking about it, leave the place you are, and find a quiet place to pray concerning the matter. By the time you return to your family, your spouse will realise what he has done and will apologise for upsetting you. But if he does not apologise, then apologise to him and move forward. I know this sounds awkward, but it is the right thing to do, because where there is love there is peace. Love is not about who is at fault and who is not at fault; it is about making everyone happy so that your home remains peacefully. When you act in a manner that brings peace, you are doing the will of God.

Once again, your marriage is suffering from domestic violence if you make angry gestures, use physical size to intimidate, shout at your spouse, destroy possessions, punch walls, wield a knife or a gun, or threaten to kill or harm your spouse and the children. If you are a person with such behaviour, seek help from God, for those who seek will find, and if you knock it shall be open unto you.

So I say to you, ask, and it will be given to you; seek, and you will find; knock, and it will be opened to you.

　　　　　　　　　　　　　　　　—Luke 11:9

For everyone who asks receives, and he who seeks finds, and to him who knocks it will be opened.

　　　　　　　　　　　　　　　　—Luke 11:10

Ten

In-Laws

X

In-Laws

Marriage is like a currency that has equal sides. It might look tremendously heavenly and euphoric on one side, but on the other side it might not be so. The bad side might be full of challenges and problems that the couple themselves could not imagine. The problems that couples experience in marriage are sometimes caused by their in-laws. In-laws can either be extremely supportive and close—or turn out to be just the opposite, causing problems in the marriage. It is a good thing to have our in-laws around, but spouses have to be careful and ensure that their presence do not affect the relationship between them and their spouse. When a man and woman get married and form a new family, they are separated from their families. The man usually leaves his parents and forms a new and stronger bond with his spouse, as this is the will of God. When a man joins his wife, he becomes the head of his wife; this means that the man now has a responsibility. His parents are no longer his responsibility. The authority is in the man's hand to exercise within his new family, and neither the man's parents nor his wife's parents are the head of the new family—they have no power to control or manipulate either the man or the wife.

> Therefore, shall a man leave his father and his mother, and be joined to his wife: and they shall become one flesh.
> —Genesis 2:24

> Wives, submit to your own husbands, as to the Lord.
> —Ephesians 5:22

For the husband is head of the wife, as also Christ is head of the Church; and He is the Saviour of the body.
                                                        —*Ephesians 5:23*

Therefore, just as the Church is subject to Christ, so let the wives be to their own husbands in everything.
                                                        —*Ephesians 5:24*

In-laws have a major role to play in marriage, but their role is not to make decisions for their son or daughter-in-law. Their duty is to be there for them, support and pray for them, and make sure that nothing goes wrong. When two people get married, their in-laws become their new family—however, this does not give in-laws the right to control the marriage. The husband still remains the head of his family and makes decisions for his new family. Some in-laws do not respect this and try to control the new family, making decisions for them as they have done in the past before their son or daughter got married. If the man allows them to continue controlling and making decisions for him and his wife, it will affect his behaviour towards his spouse and the way he takes care of things or makes decisions. It will affect the way he listens to or reasons with his wife. By allowing his in-laws to interfere in his marital life, he will cause serious problem later in the marriage.

Story 1

Ms M and her husband have been married more than two years. According to Ms M, she has no problem with her husband, but the only obstacle in her marriage is her mother-in-law. Her mother-in-law makes decisions for her husband and controls their marriage. To make things worse, his mother hired him and pays his wages. Since her husband started working for his mother, his attitude has changed. What they do or discuss within their matrimonial home is no more secret because her husband tells his mother everything. Her mother-in-law hates her and forbids her from visiting her family home and business. Her husband does not care about her but considers his parents' needs and decisions as top priority.

A lot of women experience the same thing Ms M does. A man is married to his wife and not to his mother. When a man is single he can live like a bachelor, but when he gets married he has responsibilities. He is obliged to act like a husband and lover to his wife. His parents have no right to control him, and neither do they have the right to come between him and his wife. An unattached man could allow his parents to control him, and he could remain a mummy's boy. However, things change when he becomes attached, because he is no longer unattached but joined to his wife. As an attached man, he will no longer make decisions on his own or allow his parents to make decisions for him. Every decision he makes in the family must be with his wife.

Though not all parents like the idea, spouses need not to fret concerning what their parents like or dislike—they should concentrate more on each other's needs and expectations. They should take no notice of their parents or in-laws' complaints; they must stick with each other and make decisions about how to run their lives and family. Spouses who have family business prior to their wedding ought to discuss it with their parents and let them know that their spouse will be part of it because they are their new family. Some parents might not want their son—or daughter-in-law to be part of the family business. If this is the situation, spouses must be adamant or take their own share from the business, and work in partnership with their spouse. But if spouses do not have any share in their family business, they must leave the business and plan a better future with their spouse, for that's whom they have a future with, and not their parents. When spouses work or do things together, they usually have a healthy and successful marital life.

Story 2

Mrs B and her husband have been married for more than twelve years. Mrs B's husband is a good man, but the big problem she has is her mother-in-law. Mrs B's mother-in-law complains about everything she does. She complains that Mrs B is not the right one for her son and that she regrets Mr B having chosen to marry her. She said her son and Mrs B are not old enough to make their own decisions, and that the decisions they make are always unreasonable.

She also said that Mrs B and her husband are not capable of looking after their children. She controls her son and his new family, even telling Mrs B and her husband when to have sex.

When two people decide to get married, they are saying they are ready to make decisions on their own without any interference, and even if they make mistakes or wrong decisions, they will learn from it. When it comes to children, couples have to be in charge and in control of their kids, not their parents. Though some couples do allow their parents to baby-sit their kids, this does not give their parents the right to control the marriage and children or make decisions for them. What good parents do is give their children advice without taking advantage of them. Remember, there is nowhere in the Scripture that commands in-laws to make decisions for their son—or daughter-in-law. Neither is there in the Scripture that requires mothers-in-law to control their children's marriage and sex life. Each wife has power over her husband's body; the same is true of husband.

> *The wife does not have authority over her own body, but the husband* does. *And likewise the husband does not have authority over his own body, but the wife* does.
>
> —*1 Corinthians 7:4*

A mother's presence sometimes could intimidate the daughter-in-law. A daughter might feel that while her mother is in her home, it is her responsibility to look after her mum. Though it is true that a woman has to take good care of her mother, but she must pay more attention to her husband because that is whom she is married to, and not her mother. When a husband is unable to get more attention from his wife, he will go outside to get it from another woman. When a married man starts getting attention from outside women, one day he might end up committing adultery.

Story 3

A successful footballer had an affair and his wife divorced him. He refused to admit that he was to blame for their marriage breakdown. According to him, his mother in-law helped destroyed his marriage by moving in with them and destroying the passion in their marriage. He spoke out and said 'Do not blame me, blame my mother-in-law.' His reasons was since his mother-in-law moved into their matrimonial home, their sex life became naught. He said that his sex life with his wife was virtually nothing after his mother-in-law moved in. He said, 'It was a passion killer, having your mother-in-law in the house.' The footballer claimed that his wife did not want to have sex much and used her mother's presence as an excuse. He said he never wanted her mother—in-law in the first place; but his wife put her feet down and said, 'she wanted her mum close by.'

What is this footballer saying? He is saying there was a lack of communication between him and his wife, and it was caused by her mother in-law. In other words, they could not communicate verbally and sexually, due to his mother in-law's presence in the house. Communication is very good. So, it is important that spouses communicate with each other. Where there is lack of communication in a marriage, the marriage breakdowns. Where there is no passion for making love between spouses, the marriage fails. Another way spouses can communicate in their matrimony is to have sex with their spouse. Husbands and wives must give each other what is due to them, and must not deny each other sex because love making is requisite in marriage.

> *Let the husband render to his wife the affection due her, and likewise also the wife to her husband.*
> —*1 Corinthians 7:3*

> *Do not deprive one another except with consent for a time that you may give yourselves to fasting and prayer; and come together again so that Satan does not tempt you because of your lack of self-control.*
> —*1 Corinthians 7:5*

Some mothers-in-law are hard to please, and no matter what their daughters-in-law do to make them happy; they are never satisfied and will do everything in their power to make them suffer in their matrimonial home. Things are usually this way between mothers-in-law and daughters-in-law because some men tolerate their mothers' behaviour towards their wives; they see it as something normal and put up with it. When a son permits his mother to do what she likes in his matrimonial home, she might make his wife miserable. The woman of the house might feel she does not belong to the family anymore, especially when her husband does not seem to be bothered by what his mother says or does to her.

Story 4

A woman said that her mother-in-law said things that were not true about her. When she spoke to her husband concerning his mother's behaviour towards her, he did not do anything about it because he did not see it as a problem. She also said that her husband did not what to know about the problems she was experiencing from his mother. Due to this, she did not feel like she was part of her matrimonial home. She was miserable in her marriage and felt it was time she left her husband.

> *Wherefore they are no more two, but one flesh, what therefore God has joined together, let not man put asunder.*
> —*Matthew 19:6*

Though mothers-in-law are big problem to their son's wife, they are not the only in-laws who cause problems within matrimony. Other in-laws such as a father, brother, or sister also cause huge problems. Some fathers' in-law, who do not approve their son or daughter's wedding will do anything to end their matrimony, and won't care what it takes to get rid of his son/ daughter in-law. The problems between in-laws and newlyweds are worse when a son still lives with his family after he has wed. A married man who lives with his parents should know that it cannot be possible for him to have total control of his new family whilst depending on his parents; except if he moves out of his parents' house.

Story 5

A young woman made a complaint about the way she was being treated by her sisters-in-law. According to her, her sisters-in-law hated her and made her life extremely unnerving. She lived with them and had been married to their brother for less than four years. She had a child with her husband, but her sisters-in-law did not believe that her child was their brother's. She also said that her father-in-law did not approve of her marriage to his son and therefore bribed his son to leave her. His father-in-law promised her husband that if he ended the marriage, his family would help him bring up the child.

Story 6

Mr and Mrs O have been married for more than fifteen years. Mrs O got ill, and due to her poor health, her younger sister came to live with them. When I visited Mrs O and her family, I discovered that she had been starved by her sister, who was in control of the matrimonial home. I discovered that her sister did not care if Mrs O ate. She was more interested in Mrs O's husband and was flirting with him. I also discovered that Mrs O no longer slept in the same room with her husband, and also that her sister made decisions for them. During my visit, God ministered to me to share His Word and pray for Mrs O. I shared the Word and prayed for Mrs O, as I was led by the Spirit of God. Later in the day, I prepared food for her, and for the first time in months, she was able to eat. She was so happy that she said, 'I cannot remember the last time I ate.'

In the evening, I assisted with the preparation of food for dinner. When her husband returned from work, the first thing he said to Mrs O was, 'I did not recognise you. I cannot believe this is my wife.' Mrs O responded to her husband by saying, 'I had a Godsend.' That evening she sat at the dining table and ate with her husband—this was something she had not done for a long time. Throughout my stay at Mrs O's home, she got better and no longer needed her sister making decisions and controlling her matrimonial home. She took control of her home, made decisions with her husband, did everything together with her husband, spent time with her husband, and slept with him in the same room and bed. Mrs O did not just get healed, but she also got her husband back. With God all things are possible.

> But Jesus looked at them and said to them, "With men this is impossible, but with God all things are possible.
>
> —*Matthew 19:26*

Mrs O trusted her sister and left her in charge of her matrimonial home. If she had known that her sister was not trustworthy, she would not have entrusted her with her home. What happened to Mrs O could happen to anyone. If I had never gone to visit Mrs O, her sister would have taken her husband from her. Mrs O would not have been in control because her illness took over her life. Spouses should always take control of their matrimonial home; they must not delegate authority or give control to any of their in-laws or relatives. They must dedicate their marriage to God and must commit their marital issues unto His hands. Husbands and wives should know that no problem is bigger than God Almighty. That is why He says if they call Him in the day of trouble, He will deliver them.

> Call upon Me in the day of trouble; I will deliver you, and you shall glorify Me.
>
> —*Psalms 50:15*

Story 7

Mr T and Mrs T were married for more than fifteen years and had children. Mrs T supported her husband even when he was still a student. People who knew Mr and Mrs T, wished to be like them because they were very good and accommodating. When Mr and Mrs T started to have problems in their marriage, Mr T consulted his brother, a divorcee, for some advice. His brother advised him to divorce his wife, and Mr T did. After Mr T divorced his wife, he got married to another woman, just like his brother did. At the beginning, everything looked as if it was fine for Mr T and his new wife, but later in the marriage, they started having problems—more than Mr T had had in his previous marriage. Mr T and his second wife live in the same house, but do not sleep in the same room. They hardly speak to each other. Mr T's brother, who advised him to divorce his wife; second marriage ended very badly.

> *Do not be deceived: evil communication corrupts good habits.*
> —*1 Corinthians 15:33*

> *Awake to righteousness, and do not sin; for some do not have the knowledge of God. I speak this to your shame.*
> —*1 Corinthians 15:34*

Those who have no knowledge or fear of God without doubt end their marriage and remarry when they experience marital problems. My question to those who marry and divorce is, what will they do if they divorce their spouse and marry another, and later in that marriage they experience another difficulty? Will they continue to divorce and remarry each time they have marital problems? It seems it is not a problem for some people, as they see it as their right to marry and divorce as many times they like.

Spouses who are experiencing marriage trouble must stand firm together with their spouse and resolve the issues by themselves. Spouses should not run from one relative to another seeking advice. Some relatives are good and can advise wisely when it comes to giving marital advice, but if spouses want to make their relationship work, they must have confidence in their marriage and believe in the Word of God, which says that they can do all things through Christ, which strengthens them (Philippians 4:13). Furthermore, spouses ought to know that whatever situation they face within their matrimony, God is the only solution to their problems. Those who seek advice from a divorcee will never get the solution to their problems but will end their marriage in divorce.

Divorce lawyers are evil advisers that can easily end marriages. When spouses seek advice from legal practitioners, the lawyers encourage them to divorce because they make money from it. Spouses who go to the Omnipotent get their service free, and also their marriage is restored. When spouses go to men for marriage advice, they do not get the solution to their problems. When spouses go to worldly counsellors for marriage advice, they don't get marital peace. The reason is because no man can give another peace of mind except the Prince of Peace. Jesus is the Prince of Peace, and if any man is looking for marital peace, he has to consult Christ because He is the only one that can give spouses endless matrimony peace. Furthermore, there are many men of God and counsellors all over the world, and some are chosen by God, but many are not chosen by Him. Those real men of God and counsellors who obey God and do His will; are the only people who can give couples tangible and reasonable advice that will bring a solution to their marriage problems. Spouses must be careful to whom they go for marriage advice. Spouses who are hoping for a successful and healthy marriage must look unto Jesus, the author and finisher of their faith.

> *Looking unto Jesus, the author and finisher of our faith, who for the joy that was set before Him endured the cross, despising the shame, and has sat down at the right hand of the throne of God.*
>
> —Hebrews 12:2

COUNSEL

It is so unfortunate that we cannot choose our in-laws. When you fall in love with someone and marry that person, their parents and siblings become part of your life, as they are part of the package. As families differ, so do their values, opinions, and beliefs. However, this should not cause problems between you and your in-laws. Your in-laws should always respect your opinion and the decisions you make with their son or daughter. Your spouse is your new family; some in-laws do not understand, and that is why they find it difficult to accept the new change of family. You should not belittle your spouse in front of your family, or talk down to your spouse. No matter what the disagreement is between your spouse and your family, you should always stand with your spouse.

When it comes to financial matters, do not get your parents and in-laws involved. Some families may feel that no subject is off limits. For others, it is clear that some issues are confidential and therefore only discussed between the spouses. However, it is up to you and your spouse to decide whether to discuss your private issues with your parents and in-laws, or if it is best they remain private. Whichever way you decide, make sure that your spouse is okay with the agreement. Once again, decisions in your marriage must be made between you and your spouse.

It is important that you and your spouse support each other in all the difficulties you face. Dealing with in-laws is never easy, and this is the reason why you have to be there for your spouse. Your spouse is married to you, and whatever problems she might face with your family, she will always need your support. You need to show her that your parents and siblings cannot come between the two of you and that even if they try to, you will stand by her. You should make your spouse feel that she is not alone and that you cannot be influenced by your parents. You must stand up to your parents and let them know that certain behaviour towards your spouse cannot be tolerated.

Story 8

A woman said that her mother-in-law was always unhappy with her when she failed to contact her on the phone. She said that her mother-in-law did not like her marriage to her son. She forbade her siblings and family from visiting her and warned her not to visit them. When she complained about her mother-in-law's attitude towards her, the mother-in-law called her names and said she did not get up early morning enough for house work and therefore did not deserve the food she ate and the clothes she wore. Her husband supported her mother and said to his wife that no other man would marry her, and that she was lucky to have him as a husband. Her husband demanded that they should replace her with her younger sister. Her husband said to her if she became pregnant with a girl, their marriage would be over, but if it turned out to be a boy, she could stay. Her mother-in-law verbally abused her and said to her that she was not up to the standard to be her daughter-in-law.

Spouses, your in-laws have the right to say their minds and tell you how they feel about you. However, there are limits to what they can say to you and what you can tolerate. Whatever your in-laws say or do to make you feel uncomfortable in your marriage, try to stand up for yourself. There is nothing wrong with admitting you are at fault, but there are some criticisms that are over the limit and that can be viewed as disrespectful. You do not want to cause a huge rift in the family, but you need to make it clear that you cannot be disrespected and bullied. The best way to handle such situation is to arrange a meeting between you, your spouse, and your in-laws, and explain how you feel. Tell your in-laws you love their son or daughter, and there is nothing they can do to split you up, so it is time they get on with their lives and leave you both to enjoy your marriage. Tell your in-laws that what God joins together, no one can put asunder.

> *Have you not read that He who made them at the beginning 'made them male and female'?*
>
> —Matthew 19:4

> *And said, 'For this reason a man shall leave his father and mother and be joined to his wife, and the two shall become one flesh'?*
>
> —Matthew 19:5

> *So then, they are no longer two but one flesh. Therefore what God has joined together, let not man separate.*
>
> —Matthew 19:6

Story 9

Mr E and Mrs E have been married for years without a child. They didn't argue or fight; the only problem in their marriage was Mr E's relatives. They complained about Mrs E's attitude towards Mr E and said things about her that were not true. They told Mrs E to pack her belongings and move out of her matrimonial home, if she was no longer interested in her husband. Mrs E was so upset and could not believe the way she had been treated. She was depressed and fed up with listening to her in-laws accusing her of things she never did or said. She then decided it was time she left her husband. She refused to prepare food for Mr E and told her in-laws to do it themselves.

She called me to her house and told me what had been happening in her marriage. She told me she had made up her mind that she was leaving her husband. I said to her she would look stupid if she walked out of her marriage. I advised her not to leave her husband, but she should tell him about the abuse and ill-treatment she received from her in-laws. I told her to arrange a meeting between her husband, herself, and her in-laws, because this might be the way to resolve the problems she had. I said to Mrs E that as long her husband had not asked her to leave their matrimonial home; she should pay no heed to what her in-laws said or did. She took my advice, and the meeting went very well. Today Mr E and Mrs E are happily living together and have wonderful, gorgeous kids.

Problems with in-laws are mainly due to a lack of adjustment and a lack of understanding. However, life is all about difficulties and challenges that you have to overcome. Do not walk out of your marriage because of your in-laws' mistreatment. Stay in your marriage and let your in-laws be the ones to depart. If you walk out of your marriage, your in-laws win, but if you remain steadfast, your marriage is saved. Spouses should not allow in-laws to ruin the most beautiful relationship of marriage. Be strong, be courageous, and do not be afraid, for the Lord your God is with you.

> Have I not commanded you? Be strong and of good courage; do not be afraid, nor be dismayed, for the Lord your God is with you wherever you go.
>
> —Joshua 1:9

CONCLUSION

Marriage breakdown happens as a result of all sorts of problems, some are already covered in this book. Marriage is believed to be the most intimate of relationships. It is a gift from God that should not be taken for granted. When God created Adam, he formed Eve to be his wife because he knew she would be right for him. God is the creator of every man and woman; He knew us before we were born, and He knows the right spouse for each of us. Many people pick the wrong spouse because they do not walk in the direction of the Holy Spirit. People should give their life to Christ so that they can receive the Holy Spirit. The Holy Spirit is the only one who can direct them to the right spouse.

Marriage is a commitment. People must not let a person's superficial beauty lure them to marriage. They do not want to marry someone, and then tomorrow the marriage is over. When a person is selecting a spouse, he/she must not choose a person because of outward beauty. Choose a person who is husband/wife material, who has a good moral personality.

Lack of communication is a big issue in marriage. If married couples cannot communicate due to aloofness between them, their relationships will start to go wrong. Couples should not stand and watch their marriages destroyed because of the remoteness between them. Once they start to notice the coldness in their marriage, they should speak to their spouse and find out what is wrong. If their spouse is the kind that argues each time they want to speak to them, they ought to find another way to communicate to them. Furthermore, if spouses do not communicate with each other, they will know nothing about them. However, if spouses communicate well, they will be surprised at what they can learn. They will be aware of the things that can cause problems in their marriage, and they may be better equipped to recognise when those problems occur and can deal with them efficiently.

Alcohol is a marriage breaker and a silent killer. It can affect individuals in many ways: ranging from relatively minor consequences to incapacitation and even death. The disease potentially affects everything in a person's life. A person does not have to be drunk before he accepts that he is an alcoholic. The thief does not come except to steal, kill, and destroy. Christians have to be very careful about what they eat or drink. They have to be aware of those things that the devil will use to harm their life. Jesus has come that you might have life more abundantly—that means you are fully guaranteed all of life. People's intention should be to live life to the fullest; they should not to allow the devil to destroy their lives or matrimony. They must be filled with the Spirit so that they may know when God is speaking to them, for the enemy speaks with a convincing spirit: 'It does not matter; it is only a wine or a beer, and it contains less alcohol.'

Money is a necessity, but it can be a detriment if people do not obtain it in the right manner. Money itself is not evil—it's when people start to think of evil ways to get it that it becomes evil in the eyes of the Almighty God. Although money can provide people food, shelter, education, and safety, it cannot buy love and happiness. It is easy for people to pretend to love someone or that they are happy being in a relationship. But when they are married to someone, it is a different feeling, and one day their misery will come to light. Money can buy you a lot of things, but you would not want to spend the rest of your life with someone you do not love, just so you can buy things. The eyes enjoy things of riches or wealth, and when people lust after those worldly things, it is the lust of the eyes. Christians must change their heart for God, and constantly do their best to live for Him. If Christians change their heart for the world, their desires are for the things, which the world offers, and that is the time they are guilty of the "lust of the eyes."

Love and care are two of the essential keys to a healthy and successful matrimony. If spouses do not commit to, love, and care for each other, then their marriage will become unhealthy and unsuccessful. Spouses generally experience problems in marriage. Nevertheless, love conquers all. Spouses should not look at the problems they face in their marriage; they should look at their spouse and remember the first day they met, and the day they stood before God and said 'I do.' They should remember what they said to each other, their agreed vows—that is, for better or for worse, till death do they part. This promise came from the heart and showed a genuine love from the heart, a true friendship and relationship. It showed that both of them were willing to become husband and wife, willing to face challenges and overlook faults no matter what.

The purpose of marriage is not just for husbands and wives to live together, but for both to remain truthful and faithful to each other. In a relationship where you are bound with love and care, things work simply and smoothly, and you can easily solve problems that might arise later in the marriage. Couples are supposed to motivate their spouses so that they can bring out the best in them. Spouses are also expected to do things together, to support and perfect each other. Praying together as a couple and praying individually for your spouse is one of the most powerful weapons you have against divorce and in favour of building intimacy in your marriage.

There are many gods, but there is only one God. Anybody or anything can be gods, but nobody or anything can be Almighty God. Christianity is not a religion but a revelation. It is the truth, not the untruth. It is life, not death. It is light, not darkness. It is nothing to do with idols or gods. Christianity is Christ alive in us. It means having a relationship and fellowship with Christ. The word Christian means Christ-like—that is, behaving in the manner Jesus Christ taught us. God is not religious, and neither is He part of any religion. Religions are not created by God; man did to satisfy his interest. Furthermore, the spirits that control religions do have an effect in people's lives, but in different ways. They cause huge problems between husbands and wives. Christians should not marry unbelievers or religious people (even if they think they can make them become a Christian). They should not desire to associate with religious people or do what they do. Christians must not marry an unbeliever or religious person, even if he/she promises to allow them to go to church or continue practising Christianity.

Domestic violence is one of the offensive weapons that the devil uses to destroy marriages. Domestic violence does not only destroy marriages, it also ruins the lives of the couples involved. Domestic violence is used for one purpose only: to gain and maintain total control over a spouse. The spouses who experience domestic violence sometimes do not know that they have been victims of such aggression. They think it is one of those behaviours that they have to put up with in marriage. Domestic violence is a brutal behaviour, and spouses should not tolerate such conduct. Do not ignore violence if you experience it in your marriage—seek help immediately if you notice the signs of domestic violence. Those who abuse (verbally or physically) or act violently towards their spouse will not enter the Kingdom of God.

It is so unfortunate that we cannot choose our in-laws. When you fall in love with someone and marry that person, their parents and siblings become part of your life, as they are part of the package. As families differ, so do their values, opinions, and beliefs. However, this should not cause problems between you and your in-laws. Your in-laws should always respect your opinion and the decisions you make with their son or daughter. Your spouse is your new family; some in-laws do not understand, and that is why they find it difficult to accept the new change of family. You should not belittle your spouse in front of your family, or talk down to your spouse. No matter what the disagreement is between your spouse and your family, you should always stand with your spouse. Our in-laws are part of our lives, and we want them to be there for us—but they should understand that their son or daughter has a new family, and that new family must come first.

Satan moves in a cunning way—looking for what to use to destroy happy homes. The Scripture says he is like a roaring lion seeking whom to devour. The devil ends marriages in different ways, and it does not matter to him, who or what he uses to bring an effective matrimony to an end. But whichever way the devil tries to destroy marriages, spouses must not allow it or contribute to what could make their marriage come to an end. Spouses has the power to stop the devil destroying their relationship—because God has given them power to tread on serpents and scorpions and all the powers of the enemy. Sometimes marriage problems could seem unbearable; however no matter how difficult the problems look, spouses must not give the devil the opportunity to ruin their most beautiful marital life.